SWAT Offense
11 Man

Author: Gino Arcaro
Website: www.ginoarcaro.com
email: gino@ginoarcaro.com

All rights reserved
Copyright © Jordan Publications Inc. 2012

Jordan Publications Inc.
Canada

Editor: Matthew Dawson
Design: Jessica Ingram
Design: Shelley Palomba
Design Consultant: Luciana Millone
Logistics Manager: Jordan Mammoliti
Technical Support: Leeann King

Arcaro, Gino, 1957
ISBN 978-0-9916855-2-3
http://www.ginoarcaro.com
Printed in Canada

Gino Arcaro's Story

I started lifting as a dysfunctional 12-year-old, trying to overcome my obesity. Lifting transformed my life physically and mentally. I have been lifting for over 43 consecutive years, 100% natural. I lift almost every day. It's part of who I am and it will always be, but it doesn't define me.

At 18, I started my policing career. A few years later, I became a SWAT team officer and then at the age of 26, a detective. At the same age, I accepted the head coach position at a high school, a decision that began a lengthy volunteer coaching career. I wrote my SWAT No-Huddle Offense and Defense manuals, (and recently published them) explaining the systems I had created and refined throughout 40 seasons of coaching football at the high school, college and semi-pro levels.

After 15 years, I left policing to teach law enforcement at the local college. During the next 20 years, I became a bestselling academic author, writing 6 law enforcement textbooks that are used in colleges throughout Ontario. Also during that time, I earned a Master degree, an undergraduate degree, and Level 3 NCCP Coaching certification. Then, in 2001, I opened a 24-hour gym called X Fitness Welland Inc. The gym continues to enjoy success in its second decade of operations. eXplode: The X Fitness Training System is a book I wrote that explains my workout system, based on 40+ years of lifting.

In 2010, I left teaching to make the literary transition to motivational writer. My first book, Soul of a Lifter was published in 2011. Since then, I've added several books. Blunt Talk is the name of a series I'm writing dealing with everything from fat loss to interrogation. Soul of an Entrepreneur is another series written to enlighten business owners – current and potential. In the series, 4th and Hell, I tell "David vs Goliath" tales about my Canadian club football team playing in the United States. When my first granddaughter was born, I wrote, Beauty of a Dream and the following year, I wrote Mondo piu Bello to commemorate the birth of her cousin.

I am motivated in my writing by my belief that we all have a potential soul of a lifter. We are called to lift for life. We can lift ourselves. We can lift others.

Keep lifting,

Gino Arcaro

Part 1
Technical: Passing

Chapter 1: SWAT 101

"We won't know who we are until we face pressure – the relentless kind that won't back down, bend, or break on its own. The kind that has to be faced, fought, and beaten down."

- from *Soul of a Lifter* by Gino Arcaro
www.soulofalifter.com

∞

"How we respond to fight or flight under intense pressure determines how far you go in competition, any sport, any high-risk occupation, any career, any business, and life in general. The secret to beating the odds and winning David vs. Goliath mismatches is to intensify the pressure and force a fight or flight response by your opponent. The Over 80 Rule takes over – over 80% will take flight... guaranteed."

– from *EXplode: X Fitness Training System* by Gino Arcaro
www.soulofalifter.com

∞

Item 1. There's no uncertainty with the SWAT warp-speed no-huddle. I know exactly what's going to happen – every defense does exactly the same thing.

Item 2. Every team I've coached was an underdog. If we play your team, you will have more players and they will collectively be bigger, faster, stronger, and smarter – guaranteed. My job is to weaken you.

∞

Every game we play is David versus Goliath. Not only will you have better players, you will have more resources and more preparation time. We have an unrivaled reality of limitations that may be the biggest odds to overcome in all of football anywhere on planet Earth. Here are the reasons why... the evidence to support this statement:

- Since 2004, my current team, Niagara X-Men, has been the only Canadian collegiate club team to play against American competition. We have competed against American community colleges and NCAA Division III junior varsity teams while facing overwhelming odds including:

    i. **Open-admission players – I coach Point-Zero players©** – unrecruited, second-chance, last- chance, high school graduates trying to keep their dream alive of moving to the next level.

    ii. No public funding. My wife and I pay for the team. Our gym pays the bills.

    iii. No home field. We play all our games on the road.

iv. One-man coaching staff. We have not been able to find qualified post-secondary coaches who will work for free.

v. Minimal preparation time. I have been an unpaid coach during my entire 40-season career, including 28 seasons as head coach. I have never been a full-time coach. Football coaching is my calling but I have had to work earn a living outside of football. My players are non-scholarship athletes who have to travel from 12 different cities to attend practices. They don't live on-campus or even in the same city as the practice field. Most travel between 30-120 minutes to make practice, if they have a driver's licence, if they have a car, if they don't have to work, and if they don't have class.

vi. Unmarked practice field. We cannot find a marked practice field to practice. Our markings are second-rate, giving us the worst possible look for sidelines, hash marks, and numbers.

vii. Passports. The new America passport laws have dramatically cut down our starting roster because of those unwilling or incapable of getting one.

- I've been head coach of six teams at three levels (high-school, post-secondary, semi-pro). The competitive gap has been the biggest blocker on each team… the blocker of potential that we have had to overcome each and every day of our existence. But I've asked for each mismatch. I've willing asked to have each team moved up to higher competition. We could have played at lower levels of competition but chose not to.

- We've never had a JV team.

- None of my teams have a conventional pre-season.

- None of my teams had a weight room.

- I built my own in the basement of our house in 1985 which led to a commercial 24-hour gym, X Fitness Inc., that we started from scratch in 2001.

My rookie season as a high school head coach in 1984 was a disastrous one-win nightmare. I used a ground-oriented conventional playbook. I scrapped it and started my own system from scratch. In the off season, I started designing the system that transformed our losing culture to a winning culture in one year. We recorded our first perfect season the next year in 1985.

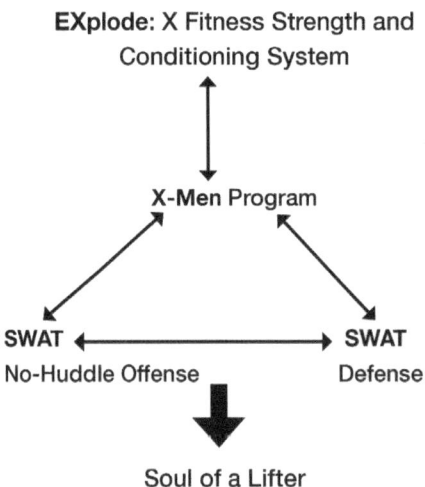

All three are connected, making the *Soul of a Lifter*. They have been responsible for over 200 **Point-Zero players**© being recruited by next level teams during forty seasons and closing David vs. Goliath competitive gaps. The EXplode: X Fitness Strength and Conditioning System builds the beast. The SWAT No-Huddle ==weakens every opponent we've ever played at any level==. The SWAT defense, uniquely connected to the offense by language, skill, and concepts is designed to force the opposing offense to do the one thing that will guarantee winning – force them to go deep.

This triple play of *EXplode X Fitness Strength and Conditioning, SWAT No-Huddle Offense*, and *SWAT Defense* didn't just happen overnight. It evolved during 40 seasons of coaching. It still is a work-in-progress.

∞

The psychology of SWAT offense is just as important as the Xs and Os. What we think and why is just as important as what we do. There are 4 SWAT tactics that are guaranteed to beat any Goliath:

1. Blitz the defense.
2. Rush the defense.
3. Enjoy the pass rush.
4. Cut down downtime.

Blitz the Defense by pressuring them harder than they attack you – and don't blink. Always send more than they send. And don't blink. Don't lose your nerve. Believe in what you're doing. And most of all, trust your training.

Defenses are conditioned to believe that they are the only unit entitled to apply pressure. Totally false. The offense can match defensive pressure and exceed it. Blitzing the defense is a change of mindset needed to achieve what we have set out to accomplish. It is impossible to run our SWAT offense without a proactive mindset because the conventional psychology of offense is reactive thinking that tends to instill fear of passing. The common football dialogue focuses on the risks of passing. Typically, the language of football is geared to create an image of the defense as being predators and the offense as potential victims. One of the keys to SWAT success is changing the language and changing the focus. The offense is not the prey waiting to be hunted. Not true. Bringing my defensive mentality to offense has been a key to SWAT success. We're an offense that thinks and plays like a defense.

I have been branded during my career as a defensive coordinator... my personality, my ideology, the type of players I attract. My reputation is a 'defense wins, offense sells tickets' attitude, even though I have never said it or even thought it. Because I believe it's a myth. My defensive coordinator experience has been the biggest influence for the *SWAT No-Huddle Offense*©. I experienced how tough it is to cover four and five receivers. I know exactly how hard it is to teach coverage skills – man and zone. I learned that pressuring the QB is the best coverage... the best passing defense. As a result, *I designed the SWAT offense as a defensive coordinator*.

We've been led to believe that the only way to protect a QB is to keep as many blockers in as possible. Maybe that's true with world-class athletes. But I don't believe it and have disproved it in our world. I have never had a QB knocked out of a game from a sack. Not once. For six years, we allowed only one sack for every 39 pass attempts. Every year, I teach and emphasize SWAT psychology from the first practice to the last. It starts with the following #1 lesson:

"I never have and never will keep the tight end in to block. And, if I have to keep both backs in to block, we are failures. If we need 2 backs and a tight end as maximum protection, let's scrap the SWAT and go back to what everyone else is doing."

That's the core message, the fundamental belief that governs the system, play-calling, and every offensive decision. This message is the way I introduce my new definition of maximum protection.

I re-defined *maximum protection*. I don't use the conventional definition of 7-8 blockers. I changed it. The SWAT definition of maximum protection is blitz the defense plus QB self-defense. Blitz the defense is our promise to block with 5 or 6. That's all we need. The most aggressive defensive coordinators we face send 5 or 6… rarely any more. And, we don't face NFL-caliber pass rushers. The only double-team pass block is a 4-rusher-versus-5-blocker situation. If it's 5-on-5, the back releases.

The onus is on the QB to protect himself – **QB self-defense** is more important than keeping 7-8 blockers to protect him. The SWAT QB self-defense philosophy includes:

- **Power Passing©**. Power running is part of the SWAT system. I started my head coaching career as a ground and pound coach – power running with running power. It worked in certain situations. As I evolved the system to include limitless passing, the pendulum swung. I became an extreme passing coach. But I had to avoid the 'finesse' label because the 'finesse' label attached to passing teams is bullshit. Complete bullshit. It's another in the long line of football myths. To avoid having my players believing the 'finesse' bullshit, I called our passing system POWER PASSING… and proved it. And we kept power running. The SWAT system includes both. **It's not just a spread offense**. The SWAT dictionary and language make the system limitless. The system can change without change. What is Power Passing? Releasing 4-5 receivers on every pass play, the threat of going deep on every play, the QB as a running threat, and the threat of reverting to power running.

- ==Power passing is blitzing the defense while maintaining the threat of running you over while you're gasping for air between plays because you can't handle the pace.== Releasing maximum (4 or 5) receivers is the #1 way for the QB to defend himself. Why? Because 100% coverage (by SWAT definition) of 4-5 receivers won't happen. And we have film evidence to prove it. At least 2 receivers will be open, by our definition, on every play. If the speed limit is broken.

- A back releasing is better than a back blocking. As stated, I coach players from scratch. It's challenging enough to teach backs to be a ballcarrier, run routes, and catch passes under pressure. Adding blocking doesn't fit my curriculum – no time, no coaches. That's not a cop-out. It works. I don't want mismatched backs trying to block over-sized pass rushers and likely lose each battle.

- There's at least one hot receiver on every play. Protect yourself by throwing to him.

- The QB is a ballcarrier who throws. This mindset protects the QB from believing he is fragile. I never teach a QB to "scramble" – he is taught how to run, when, why, and where. The QB as a ballcarrier mentality.

- Go deep. Every time you complete a deep pass, you're forcing pass rushers to run long distances to get to the LOS. **Long distance running adds up.** It forces the defense to do what is unnatural to them. Even incomplete long passes forces the cover defenders to run long distances. **Never forget the amount of yards the defense has to run back to the LOS.**

- Rush the defense. Speeding up the game, slows down the pass rush.

Rush the Defense by speeding up the game physically and mentally de-mystifies any defense at any level. Breaking the speed limit solves every defensive mystery. Rushing the defense causes any defense at any level to unravel. Rushing the defense makes them dysfunctional. They will not be aligned and not be ready for action. Rushing the defense weakens their will, limiting them strategically, softening the strongest of defenses. Quarterbacks and receivers easily read predictable coverage. The SWAT No-Huddle slows any defense's pass rush to a jog. Rushing the defense lets us rush the defense… on the ground. We can't ground and pound a well-rested Goliath. The fastest way to develop our ground attack is to rush the defense by softening their core.

Enjoying the Pass Rush is the secret to high-octane passing. Everything else is secondary. Enjoying the pass rush is the winning QB mindset… the attitude needed to make it happen. It's not optional. It's impossible to build an explosive air attack. Enjoying the pass rush has a dual meaning:

(i) **Pass rush anxiety** is the biggest reason for passing failure. Pass rush anxiety is the greatest obstacle in QB development. It's impossible to win without curing pass rush anxiety. The defensive pass rush is the biggest threat to both the QB and the entire passing system. Coverages are secondary. Coverages don't ground the QB, the pass rush does. Coverages are not the biggest threat. Anticipation of harm is worse than the harm itself. Anticipation of pain is stronger than the actual pain. Anticipation of the pass rush is the best defensive strategy in the history of football.

The pass rush triggers one of 3 F-Bombs© that lead to an implosion or explosion – freeze, flight, or fight. The first two are manifestations of fear. The third reveals fearlessness. Flight does not refer to all QB running. The SWAT offense depends heavily on the QB running as a ballcarrier. Flight means randomness… running before it's time to run, running without purpose. Structured QB running within the context of a warp-speed, multi-formation offense is a knockout punch. Freeze is worse than flight – it creates a stationary target. Fight means a change of focus. The QB's focus has shifted away from the pass rush to his receivers. The frightened QB becomes frightening. The frightening QB is the greatest threat to the defense.

A QB cannot function while focusing on the pass rush. Focus on the pass rush is the leading cause of QB dysfunctionalism. A winning QB enjoys the pass rush instead of fearing it. The key is changing the QB's mindset toward the pass rush from pain to pleasure. The QB must perceive the pass rush as a challenge, not an obstacle. Change the focus, change the outcome. What you focus on grows.

(ii) The second type of pass rush anxiety is performance demand anxiety, referring to fear of intense responsibility. Contrary to popular myth, QBs and receivers don't always love pass-oriented systems. The "I-want-the-ball" bravado often disappears when reality sinks in and they're required to pass and catch the ball a lot. Suddenly, 'wanting' the ball doesn't seem appealing. Like in all professions, there's a love-hate relationship with heavy workloads. Being the star sounds good but sometimes the demands of stardom are a crushing weight. Not all QBs and receivers want the responsibility of throwing 50-60 times per game or having 15-20 passes thrown at them every game. The SWAT warp-speed no-huddle annually separates those who want the ball and those who need the ball. Those who need it get the *pass rush – the adrenaline rush* from the challenge of extraordinary performance demands of high-octane passing. Those addicted to the pass rush become unstoppable forces. Those who don't, never get off the ground.

Cutting Down Downtime is reverse clock management. We don't conserve time, we don't waste time, we don't kill the clock. SWAT clock management is the opposite of conventional strategy – we extend the clock, lengthening the game instead of shortening it. Our clock management objective is the Over 80 rule –we strive to run a minimum of 80 offensive plays. A double-header. Our team record is 105 offensive plays versus Alfred State College (Alfred, New York) in 1998 without one college age player on the team. Fifty in the first half, fifty-five in the second half. The Over 80 Rule has three reasons/benefits:

1. Defenses cannot shut down over 80 plays.

2. More scoring opportunities.

3. More reps to develop players.

My primary mission is to develop players. That's why my team exists. **Over 80©** translates into double the game reps. We use the same tempo during practice – train like you fight, fight like you train. Double the practice experience, double the game experience. My *EXplode X Fitness Strength and Conditioning* system is compatible with the no-huddle tempo. We cut down downtime during workouts, changing the rest-work ratio to match the demands of our warp-speed no-huddle.

Rush the Defense and You Sack the Defense. Increasing the pass rush decreases the pass rush. Rushing to throw more passes faster slows down pass rushers. Speed up the tempo of the passing game is a security management tactic – it protects the quarterback. The SWAT system routinely pumps out 300- 600 passing yards per game. I believe in the power of stretch goals. Stretch goals are forces of nature. We demand them and reach them. Six hundred passing yards is only one example. The number one reason we reach this stretch goal is the low number of QB sacks we give up. We keep the QB standing even with inferior blockers. We have never had an offensive line that has been physically dominant, more experienced, or more skilled than our opponent. But our QB security and protection is top-notch – because the defense lays off physically, mentally, and strategically.

Defenses develop an inner clock that matches the play clock. Throw their inner clock out of whack and they stop playing like they are trained to play. They lose their identity. Defenses play exactly like a strength training workout – 8-1 rest-work ratio. About five seconds of work followed by about forty seconds of rest. Defenses are addicted to downtime. They are hooked on long rest periods between downs. We dramatically change the work-rest ratio to 1-2... about sixteen seconds of work to eight seconds rest. That's how we train on the field and in the gym. We train by cutting down downtime.

Downtime is the time between downs (or sets in the gym). Take away the defense's rest and recovery time and their defenses drop. Defenses go into withdrawal – literally and figuratively. Playing without the normal rest and recovery is painful for the defense because the high-speed tempo takes the defense out of their comfort zone, into their discomfort zone, and into slower man-to-man coverage. If a tired defense stays in any zone, we slice them up.

Cut down downtime and the defense will withdraw their game plan, their strategy, their tenacity, their speed, their skill, and their execution. Defensive withdrawal symptoms reveal in predictability – alignment and assignment stay the same. Every defense does the exact same thing. *Defenses limit themselves while we become unlimited.* We go in different directions. Knowing what every defense will do when we rev up the game is my biggest advantage to offset our disadvantages.

First, one game plan fits all. ==The SWAT system is the game plan for every opponent==. Having to work for a living outside football limits my film study time. Even with film study, I designed a SWAT system where the system is the game plan. I developed a play-calling concept that I call *Strategize and Improvise©* – general plan and adapt to the situation. I learned this in frontline policing, used it in teaching, and in business. *Strategize and Improvise©* is a play-calling concept that lets me survive as a Point-Zero coach – a one-man coaching staff, an outsider who doesn't coach football full-time, who coaches open-admission second-chance players. Secondly, I don't have to teach the QB how to read coverage until he's mastered the SWAT system because: (a) there's no immediate need – defenses use the same coverage when they're rushed; and (b) the SWAT system consists of partial pass concepts that are both zone-busters and man-busters. We play our game, not theirs.

The *EXplode X Fitness Strength and Conditioning©* is the core of SWAT success. The reason is hybrid training. The human body is a miracle hybrid machine – three energy systems. *EXplode* trains all three by focusing on sustained workload and lifting 225 lbs for both bench press and squats. Defenses are conditioned to use only one energy system. SWAT players are energy efficient. Most defenses are energy deficient. That's the true secret of the SWAT success. In addition to perfect seasons and championships that started with pre-season hopelessness, the three best examples of SWAT success are three individual single-game performances that were recognized by Sports Illustrated's Faces in the Crowd in a three-year span:

#1. **1998 – QB passed for 836 yards, 8 TDs, and 6 two-point conversions in a 66-51 win against a first-place team. He later became a two-time winner of Canada's version of the Heisman.**

#2. **1998 – In his first game as a starter RB, versus a defending championship team, rushed for 369 yards on 20 carries, scoring 6 TDs and 3 two-point conversions and one interception playing cornerback, in a 54-6 win.**

#3. **2001 – WR caught 9 passes for 186 yards, scored two TDs, intercepted 3 passes for 82 yards, returned one punt for 58 yards, and recovered an onside kick.**

Iron-man strength and conditioning – going for it on 4th down, going for two, onside kicks... these three case studies tell the SWAT and *EXplode* story.

∞

My offensive game plan is the same every game – wear down the defense, break their will, maximize ball distribution to players and field, and go deep.

Going Deep is in our DNA. We re-defined deep as: (a) any pass that does not travel short (under 10 yards), and (b) every single pass we throw, regardless of air time, is intended to go deep with yards after the catch (YAC). We prefer to have every pass caught during a full sprint instead of a stationary target. And we consider the reception-point to be the start of a running play – an organized running play with structured downfield blocking.

Maximum Ball Distribution means we want every receiver catching passes. No decoys. If you're on the field, we throw to you. And we want to throw to every square inch of the field or at least run patterns there. We force the defense to cover the entire field – vertically, horizontally, and behind the LOS.

Maximum Muscular Failure (MMF) is the way to wear down a defense and break their will. As the needle gets closer to E, defenses are not ready to play physically or mentally. Not ready to play is the physical evidence we look for. When the defense does not align properly, we blitz harder. Training the hybrid makes us stay stronger longer. That's the secret to beating Goliaths.

∞

Policing taught me the power of rapid decision-making (RDM). Making calls in the blink of an eye is a force of nature. Processing volumes of information and making a call at lightning speed is a game-breaker. It tilts the playing field against any Goliath. RDM is a science that doesn't just happen. It needs hundreds of thousands of simulated reps and practical experience. You can't learn it on demand. When fully developed, RDM is an explosive constructive force. Untrained, the pressure of having to make rapid decisions is a crushing force.

The SWAT system forces the game to become a battle of RDM.

∞

The difference between winning and losing is your definition of hard work.

The SWAT and *EXplode* systems are built on one core belief – the surefire way to beat the odds is to have a better definition of hard work than your opponent. 'Hard work' is an abstract concept that gets defined differently. Those who define hard work the best and practice it the most, win. Those who don't, lose.

The goal of the SWAT system is to outwork every opponent by making a performance challenge – ==challenge the other team to work harder than they have trained.== Challenge them to go places inside their minds that they never visited. By challenging the opponent to work harder than their training, you will guarantee winning for one simple reason – ==it's impossible to out-perform training. It's impossible to perform at a higher level than you train for.==

The level of training sets the limit for game performance, physically and mentally. It's impossible to cross the training threshold in a game. The only way to raise the bar is to train harder before the next game. This is the secret to beat Goliaths – force them to cross a higher threshold of work and pain than they're capable of... and they won't because they can't. Crossing a higher threshold doesn't just happen. It has to be developed through ==next-level, threshold-crossing reps==. If defenses are not consistently incorporating next-level, threshold-crossing reps during practice, they will never raise the bar. They won't improve. They can be beaten if the offense lays down the gauntlet by crossing the threshold and challenging the defense to do the same.

If your breaking point is higher than your opponent's, you can beat any Goliath. And you will.

This rule has never failed. When we successfully challenge the opponent to work harder than they have trained, the opponent breaks – guaranteed. When we fail to issue that challenge, we lose – guaranteed.

The key is accurately defining hard work and then living it. Whoever does a better job will win. Hard work tilts any playing field – balanced or unbalanced.

The SWAT and *EXplode* systems are built on pressure and extreme hard work. Extreme strength and conditioning. My job is to weaken the opponent through the concept of fatigue mismanagement – force them to mismanage discomfort and pain through the wonder of fatigue.

Fatigue is the strongest ally for the David versus Goliath match-ups. Fatigue cuts through the bigger, faster, stronger. Ordinary fatigue won't cut it. Extraordinary fatigue is needed. Extraordinary fatigue starts at the top, in the opponent's mind. Show the defense uncertainty... the unfamiliarity of a warp-speed offense that throws limitless formations and blitzes the defense relentlessly. Fatigue mismanagement is the great equalizer. It's the secret weapon that allows any David to beat any Goliath.

And you need five smooth stones.[1] **Blitz the defense with 5 receivers every 8 seconds.** We throw intense pressure at the defense until it breaks. We are not a typical no-huddle. We break every speed limit, use every formation imaginable, throw to every square inch of the field, throw to every receiver... without a conventional playbook. All this done by building plays at the LOS at lightning speed. The SWAT offense is a warp-speed no-huddle that you can't prepare for. It's impossible for opponents to simulate the SWAT system because of:

(i) Unwillingness. The sustained work we force the defense to do physically and mentally will never be replicated in any practice because players will revolt or quit. Prominent university recruiters on both sides of the border have told me this after watching our practices to scout players; and

(ii) No time. There is not enough practice time to prepare for the volume of formations and pass plays we use each and every game. You cannot fully prepare to shut down a limitless system.

∞

The *SWAT No-Huddle Offense*© is a system that doesn't coach elite athletes – it makes them... from scratch. It's a one-of-a-kind offensive system guaranteed to work out. The *SWAT No-Huddle Offense*© is the most unique offensive system because it doesn't have a conventional playbook, it has limitless passing, it connects with the SWAT no-playbook defense, and it has worked on both sides of the border for three decades. The secret is connecting partial concepts at warp-speed that can build any formation, any pass play, and any running play to fit the situation, at the line of scrimmage without a conventional playbook that has to be memorized. Memorization is replaced by translation of a language.

I designed the SWAT offense as a solution to a nightmarish reality of limitations, the most extreme adversity imaginable – **playing in poverty.** Poor talent, poor resources. One-man coaching staff, no junior varsity teams, minimum finances, open-admission players, horrible practice fields, and out-matched opponents... willingly. I have been an unpaid head coach of six teams at three levels – high school, collegiate, and semi-pro – without having had the luxury of coaching full-time. My preparation time has been limited because of paid occupations and running two businesses. And I willingly moved each team to the highest possible competitive levels — David constantly calling out Goliath.

None of my teams had a winning culture when I became head coach. Each team was either stuck in a losing culture or was brand new... start-up teams without winning traditions. My current team, Niagara X-Men, is a non-profit collegiate club team funded privately by my wife and I – no public funding, no government assistance... Canada's only collegiate club team to play against American post-secondary competition. All on the road. No home field. One-man coaching staff. A roster of twenty-something competing against rosters of **Over 80©**.

---

1   Tribute to a masterpiece. *"Then he took his staff in his hand, chose five smooth stones from the stream, put them in the pouch of his shepherd's bad and, with his sling in his hand, approached the Phillistine."* 1 Samuel 17:40.

All six of my teams have transformed from losers to winners. The transformation starts in the weight room, works its way to on-field conditioning, and then to our paperless, limitless offense and defensive system that survive on one concept – relentless pressure. Our defense blitzes offenses from traditional to extremely unconventional formations. We relentlessly blitz the defense until they limit themselves. As the defense's limits grow, our limits disappear.

Our goal has been to develop **Point-Zero Players©** to the next-level… developing players from scratch to get recruited to post-secondary and beyond. One way to achieve this goal is to dramatically increase game experience by **increasing the number of plays and not ignoring simplicity.** It's worked. During my 40-season coaching career, the system has developed over 200 players who were recruited by the next- level. Those who have not been recruited chose not to be. Free will was exercised.

Another unique feature is the **offense-defense connection** – the SWAT offense and SWAT defense are connected. The reasons are our need for two-way player depth and only one coach to teach it. Not only are two-way starters a necessity, so are two-way second and third stringers. Every starter must learn another position to build an effective depth chart. Consequently, I blended as much SWAT language, decision-making, and technique as possible. Example: a partial passing concept used in our base stretch pass called the high-low cross also serves as a high-low blitz bind.

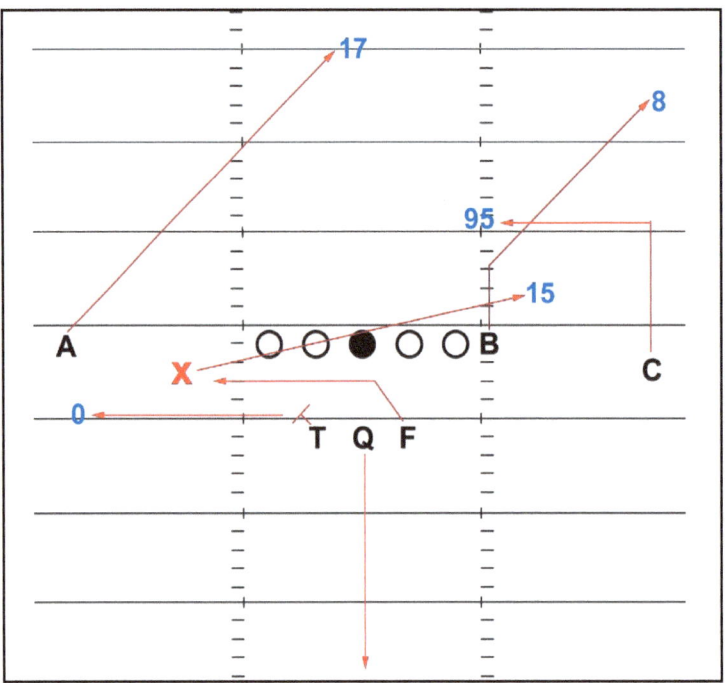

This diagram shows our **base stretch pass**. The A and X receivers run a High-Low Cross partial passing concept (17 and 15 respectively in the SWAT dictionary). This partial passing concept is exactly the same as a partial blitz concept used by a defensive end and inside linebacker/strong safety. The code names (Alpha and X-Ray) are exactly the same for both offense and defense. These are two examples that show the connection between the offense and defense in the SWAT system.

Instead of celebrating winning and grieving losing, study them. That's how discoveries are made. That's how we find a better way… a simpler way. That's how we find what really works in each of our unique realities. I didn't study NFL QBs or Heisman candidates. I studied our Point-Zero

QBs. REPS – Research Every Practice Set. I don't differentiate between practice and game. Our practices and games look exactly the same. Every play we execute is practice to get better, whether it's in a game or practice. I group plays/drills into sets, like workouts. Single-sets and supersets. Research every set to find out why things happen and you'll make startling discoveries. Mine led to **QB Psychology 101.**

My biggest discovery that transformed the SWAT offense was how our QBs found open receivers. Twenty years ago, the discovery of open-receiver-discovery impacted the entire SWAT system. It prompted me to replace the phrases "primary receiver", "secondary receiver", and "high, low, check down to backs" with the Board Theory:

>see the whole board
>
>know the situation
>
>make the call
>
>remember it

After experimenting with several read progressions, by numbering intended receivers from one to five, I discovered that QBs find open receivers differently than I had thought and taught. QBs see a board, like a chess player sees the pieces on a chessboard. When they see the board, they try to recognize images formed first by receivers alone and then by both receivers and defenders. Receivers versus air, then receivers in a crowd. That influenced my teaching progression.

Every pass play forms a unique image. Every time a QB sees the image, it gets burned deeper and deeper into long-term memory. Eventually, the miracle of reps does its magic – quarterbacking becomes automatic. The force of second nature. There's the secret that developed **SWAT Point-Zero QBs** into 300-600-yard passers.

The whole board that QBs see at one time is one of three 90-degree angle fields-of-vision:

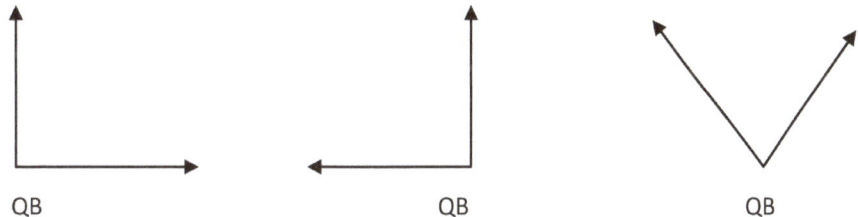

These became the three frontsides for pass plays. The more evenly spaced receivers on the frontside, the more pieces on the board. The more the QB sees a similar image, the more he remembers and recalls that image. And when the image is burned, the QB can recognize open receivers better and faster – accurate identification of open receivers in the blink of an eye.

Nothing is more important to our offense than the QB finding open receivers. Nothing is harder to teach. And nothing is harder to learn. The reason is threat and risk. No football player has to deal with more relative threat and risk than a Point-Zero QB. No player has to overcome more pressure – physically, intellectually, emotionally – than a rookie QB. No one. If a QB can't find open receivers, nothing else matters.[2]

---

2 Tribute to a masterpiece. *Nothing Else Matters* by Metallica. Our program lifts heavy metal to a wide range of music but no music

I learned that Point-Zero QB development starts at the top – in the mind. QB mind-set is the single-most important factor in the SWAT system. It affects the entire team – not just the offense... defense as well. Faith in the QB is the catalyst of our team performance. There is a direct relationship between team confidence in the QB and winning and losing. When we believe in the QB, we win. When we don't, we lose. Football is obviously a team sport but positions are not created equal. That's why QB Psychology is my priority, not because of preferential treatment, teaching it connects to every other football skill. Coaching football alone has its advantages – I learned to connect "indy" time into superset drills that teaches multiple position-skills and conditioning... all stemming from QB Psychology.

Two factors are guaranteed to dramatically improve the QBs finding of an open receiver:

(i) **re-defining going deep.** Equality of routes – all routes are intended to go deep. Knowing that his receivers have the willingness and capacity to gain significant yardage after every catch; and

(ii) **focusing on the right rush.** Focus on the internal pass rush, not the external pass rush.

When I re-defined "going deep," a transformation happened to our passing game. A performance explosion happened. Yards piled up. Yards translate to points. The reason was confidence of knowing that NO PASS COMPLETION IS WRONG. Regardless of situation, no completed pass is the wrong call. The only wrong that can happen is not gaining enough yards after the catch. The length of the actual pass is not the primary issue. The distance that the ball travels is not our top priority. What matters is completing the pass and gaining yards after the catch. The moment we changed the focus, the curtain lifted, the ceiling raised. **Knowing the situation** is vital to building a pass play by positioning as many receivers in the same QB sight line and a bonus to select the right receiver... but in theory, the situation doesn't dictate the receiver because every receiver is expected to either make a first down or score.

In our system, a short pass in a long situation is not wrong. A long pass in a short situation is not wrong. The only wrongs are failing to find an open receiver, failing to complete a thrown pass, failing to convert a completed pass to a first down or touchdown with yards after the catch. Reducing the needless stress of making the wrong call regarding receiver selection opened the air waves. Our rule is simple – **no open receiver is the wrong choice.** Regardless of situation, every receiver is the right call as long as he is open by our definition.

Our definition of 'open' starts with a negative – not 100% covered. Then the definition continues contextually by answering on split-second question: have you completed a similar pass before. Those are the two parts of the definition. If the receiver is not 100% covered, meaning impossible for that receiver to make the reception, then the quarterback's IQ takes over – Instinct Quotient. A high IQ is a jacked instinct – lean and mean. Low IQ is a weak, out-of-shape instinct that barely has a pulse. High IQ is a powerful force – muscle memory with a soul. Strong instinct is more than a hunch or gut feeling, it's a defense mechanism. High IQ is an inner force that flips the survival-mode internal switch at the perfect moment. Strong instinct is a trained impulse built by intense training and practical experience – a radar warning device equipped with a firing mechanism.

The Board Theory and High IQ are connected. Reps at seeing the board at live speeds lift the IQ score one digit at a time.

---

has had a greater influence on our training than Metallica.

Starting on Day 1 of SWAT 101, I teach that every SWAT pass is intended to go deep. No exception. There are no 'short passes' in the system. Instead, there are long-distance plays, defined as: (a) long-distance passes, and (b) short-distance passes followed by long-distance run. **Change the mindset, change the outcome. M.O.** – **M**indset is connected to **O**utcome. Language influences performance. 'Short pass' gets short results. It's not enough to tell receivers to earn yards-after-catch. It has to be taught and conditioned, starting with psychology and physical reps that simulate the expected outcome. The best example is the concept of long-distance run after every catch. Not one pass is caught in practice without some length of long-distance pass. Not against air, not against defenders. No receiver ever catches a pass, stops, and casually returns to the LOS flipping the ball to someone while jogging or walking back to the waiting-line to spectate the next drill. Every pass caught is followed by a sprint to a whistle – no exception. Train like you fight, fight like you train. Every rep is an investment into a positive or negative return. Don't tolerate in practice what is not tolerated in a game. Every year, rookie receivers have to be re-wired. Every year, I teach my long-distance sprint-to-the-whistle rule, in writing and off-season communication. But bad habits are tough to break. No matter how many times I teach rookies before the first practice, they're past dictates the present. They stop as soon as they catch the pass. That's the most powerful teaching moment for a receiver. It's corrected instantly. Immediate transformation. Every rookie fights for long-distance **y**ards-**a**fter-**c**atch (**YAC**).

How do you increase YAC? Fatigue brought on by offensive pass rush. Drain the defensive battery and two things drop: coverage and pursuit. Once they fall behind, the race becomes a mismatch that not even a Goliath can handle.

Focusing on the right rush is the secret to QB success by whatever definition is attached to it. A QB will never successfully execute the SWAT system unless he changes his focus from the external defensive pass rush to the inner adrenaline rush of the challenge. Once the QB ignores the defensive pass rush, he becomes a beast – guaranteed. There's only one way to complete the QB makeover and change his focus: **REPS** – **R**epeated **E**xposure to **P**ressure and **S**tress©. I learned this secret in frontline policing. No one is born fearless. No one is born gutless. Both are developed through experiences and rewards. What is not experienced will never manifest. It's impossible to perform what has never been experienced. The value of any experience depends on its reward. What gets reinforced, catches on. What is not reinforced, is dropped. This is why I don't buy red vests for QBs. This is why I don't coddle QBs. This is why I simulate games during every rep of every practice – down, distance, hash mark, game clock, play clock, score… 100% simulation. Live. And that's why I have never had a QB injured in practice. Not one missed rep because of a practice injury. QBs are tougher than we give them credit for and they become masters at self-defense only when they face real REPS. Half-assed, half-speed reps alone will never fully build a QB's potential. I never have and never will shelter QBs from pressure and stress during practice because of the evidence. I'm not referring to subjecting the QB to senseless, repeated violence. But they have to hear the word "live." It's impossible to go "live" on demand during games without having trained for it. We become what we rep-out. We don't become what we don't rep. Reps are not created equal. There are challenging reps and unchallenging reps. Both have merit but there's a difference between the two. Unchallenging reps maintain – they make you stay the same… at best. Challenging reps make you grow. My teaching goal is to constantly raise the bar – lift the quantity and quality of challenging reps. With the right challenging reps, there is no limit to QB development – Point-Zero to 600 in 60 minutes.

The true measure of a team is what it does with a struggle – crush it or get crushed. Triumph over struggle or be defeated by it. The difference between winning and losing is the response to struggle. My goal at every practice and every workout is to create struggle and build their will to beat it. The value of every set and every superset is the intensity of the struggle – the degree of difficulty. No struggle, no forward progress. Train like you fight, fight like you train. Train soft, fight soft. Train hard, fight hard.

∞

Thinking 40-time is more important than running 40-time. How fast pressured, tired players can think is directly related to winning. How fast fully-rested, pressure-free untested players can run 40 yards in a straight line is not directly related to winning. Thinking speed under intense pressure and time constraints is far more important than fully-rested 40-times under perfect conditions. The SWAT system teaches how to play outside your comfort zone... in the discomfort zone. The X factor that separates winning from losing is how discomfort is handled... performance under stress and distress. Playing when conditions aren't perfect. The inability and unwillingness to work through discomfort is the leading cause of losing.

Other than for the purpose of structured team combines that I conduct for next-level recruiting, I have never timed players in 40-yard sprints for actual practice and never will. The reason is relevance. I have found no direct relevance between non-fatigued 40-times and winning with a warp-speed no-huddle. What matters in the SWAT system is who is faster after the effects of intense work start messing up the mind and body. What matters in the SWAT system is how much you can take... how much intellectual pressure and how much physical pressure. Until they remove all violence and contact from football, handling mental and physical pressure is the single-most important element that separates winning from losing. Pressure doesn't mean just a tight game at the two-minute warning. Pressure refers to the forces that try to break you to pieces every second of every game... the crushing weight that either gets lifted or busts you up.

I replaced conventional 40-times with 8-second thinking-ratio – the blue-collar formula. Consistent 8-second rapid-decisions followed by 8-seconds of physical work. A 1-1 ratio. I learned this during my high school flour mill job – eight hours of intense physical and mental pressure brought on by having to exert extreme strength and energy every 8 seconds. This extreme workload built the blue-collar worker – blue-collar armour... blue-collar mindset and blue-collar body. It built the 90-10 Rule – 90% got cut, 10% survived the cut. True Athletic Darwinism. ==A blue-collar culture guarantees winning==. Never fails. There's a direct relationship between blue-collar armour and winning. Building the blue-collar wins. Not building it, loses. The blue-collar promise is the true secret of winning.

The SWAT system has blue-collar DNA. The Xs and Os are secondary. The intention of the system is to build blue-collar 40-times, those who can out-run, out-think, and out-work any Goliath during a battle of sustained pressure. The real litmus test of speed is **4th-quarter 40-yard sprint times**. Not one sprint, but an unbroken chain of sprints that produce 75% fatigue. 75% is the equivalent to 3 played quarters. What matters is:

- how long can you stay strong?

- how fast can you last?

- what happens when three-quarters of the game is gone?

The single-most embarrassing experience I can think of is the dreaded 4th-quarter collapse. It's an indictment on every aspect of your program from coaching and playing, it discloses every physical and mental muscle fiber or lack thereof. **Fourth-quarter performance has a soul of its own.** Look deeply at the 4th quarter performance and you'll see the soul of the team and its coach.

You don't need a stop watch to measure 4th-quarter speed – just observe. Watch for two things – the gap between ballcarrier and defender, then turn to the scoreboard. When we build blue-collar receivers, blue-collar backs, blue–collar lineman, blue-collar QBs, we win big. When we don't, we lose big.

$$\infty$$

∞Reps© (Infinite Reps) is the true secret of success by whatever definition you attach to it.

It's fashionable to be searching for the secret to success and fulfillment, the magic formula to winning, or new wave short cut to riches. There is no path of least resistance. Resistance training on the field and in the gym is a guaranteed strategy to building the beast to survive in any high-risk activity or job. The key to any Resistance Training is a force that has to be fought through – weight that has to be lifted, defenders who have to be blocked and outrun, and time constraints... reps versus air can and must be faced with resistance through pressure of an second 8-second time clock for both thinking and working. Short rest, long rep. Limit play-calling to 8 seconds but extend every practice rep to 8 seconds minimum. The secret to increasing big plays is to increase big-play reps. Big plays don't just happen. They are a by- product of your reps. Every drill, every play in practice lasts a minimum of 8 seconds. No quick whistles. Running plays, short passes, deep passes all have to break the 8-second work barrier. The psychology of work. That's how strong work ethic is built. Long reps and infinite reps – ∞Reps.

No one is born with a strong work ethic. It doesn't just happen mysteriously. Strong work ethic has to be built. It has to be taught, learned, and most-importantly experienced – felt deep inside. There has been a serious decline in work ethic among the student-athletes who I've coached on the field and taught in college lecture halls. The decline has had two turning points: the end of 1998 and middle of 2005. The first one coincided with the explosion of the World Wide Web a few years after it entered the scene. The middle of 2005 coincided with the growing popularity of social media, cell phones, laptops, video games and all other mobile electronic addictions. I am not a technology-bashing dinosaur. But technology is not a toy and it's addictive for those who use it without a purpose and meaning. Add the lack of parental leadership and growing substance abuse in high school and post-secondary and you have a work-ethic crisis. It's not a small problem, it's severe. When I was a cop between 1975-1990, I witnessed shocking self-destructive social behaviour – adults and adolescents alike. When I became a high school head coach in 1984, my attitude toward football changed dramatically. I realized that I was not simply coaching Xs and Os – I was changing behaviour. I stopped viewing football from a fan's perspective. My favourite pro football team's success was no longer a source of instant gratification. Suddenly, I learned that the biggest reward was not living vicariously through professional athletes and professional coaches. The biggest reward was putting up ladders for Point-Zeros. I realized that coaching amateur football is one of the most important jobs on planet Earth because of the endless capacity to make positive impacts on Point-Zero lives. Nothing else I have done comes close to it. Policing certainly makes a positive impact but the occupation is largely about helping clean up social messes of shattered lives and then leaving. College teaching makes a tremendous positive impact but there's a limit because there's no experience of team concept... the power of unifying hearts, minds, and souls in one direction to achieve one common purpose is missing. Business and writing have the potential to change lives but the quality of the sacred memorable experience that only coaching football can evoke is not the same. The type of impact a football coach can make is unmatched.

The true secret to building a blue-collar work ethic is ∞Reps – infinite reps. Limited reps, limited performance. ∞Reps is the only high-yield investment that guarantees a winning return. Each rep makes anything easier and easier until it becomes automatic. Then change the reps – make them harder. The concept of infinite reps is a chain of ordinary reps followed by extraordinary reps – unchallenging reps followed by challenging reps. Ordinary, unchallenging reps build the base. Extraordinary, challenging reps move you to the next level. And there are infinite levels of performance. Contrary to popular belief, performance is not neatly separated into rookie and veteran or beginner, intermediate, and expert. There are infinite performance levels between Point-Zero and expert, each one a step on the ladder to reaching the highest level of performance of potential. This applies both to players and teams. Self-actualization of players and teams depends on an unbroken chain of base-building reps that stabilize performance and next-level reps that lift performance. This 2-step rep process applies to each performance level – same reps, then change the reps. That's how the SWAT offense grows. Breaking the chain or reversing it stagnates the offense. Rep-consistency is key. Like sleep deprivation, you can't catch up on lost reps.

Can you win with bad reps? Yes, if the opponent trained with weak reps also. But, eventually inferior, mediocre reps catch up to you.

$$\infty$$

The strongest opponent to the SWAT warp-speed no-huddle is not a specific defensive formation or specific coverage or specific blitz. The worst enemy is laziness. Apathy and lethargy will ground the SWAT offense like no defense can.

Laziness is contagious. It spreads through a team like a virus. The leading cause is iron deficiency — no gym reps at all or bad gym reps. Off-field and on-field workout laziness is a mask that disguises the desire to take the path of least resistance. There's a growing notion among high school players that they have arrived… that practice is a necessary evil, a ritual but not a necessity. More and more high school players are being told they are the greatest and more and more believe it. Humility is harder to find than an open receiver under a heavy pass rush. Intolerable attitudes are on the rise. The threat of laziness has reached an all-time high.

If your team is losing, do an inventory of the team's inner self and you will positively find twin negative forces of lazy mind and lazy body. Lazy thinking and lazy action. Left unchecked, it'll spread through your offense. Protecting your team with the strongest virus protection is essential to prevent a crash.

What has stopped SWAT? Me. I got soft during the last couple of seasons. Compromised my promise of zero tolerance for laziness. I ignored what I never ignored in the past. I tolerated what never was tolerated. The result was a string of embarrassing games that grounded the SWAT offense for the first time. I learned to never complain about what you tolerate. Instead, I returned to zero tolerance. That's the key to the SWAT system – zero tolerance for laziness.

$$\infty$$

How a system is taught is just as important as what is taught.

The SWAT system is not a playbook. It's a philosophy and ideology, a new psychology, with a unique pedagogical approach. How the SWAT system is taught is just as important as the Xs and Os. But, how something is taught goes beyond words, more than words. There's an energy communicated during live coaching that cannot be duplicated in writing. It's impossible to fully explain how to teach passion with 100% accuracy in a book. No book can fully re-create an experience. Something's always lost when an experience that has to be felt deep down is explained. Written stories always fall short of the real thing. More than written words are needed. There's nothing like the real thing. But, as a close second place, I will be posting videos to supplement this book.

My teaching plan starts by explaining **SWAT 101**. The SWAT system is limitless. SWAT 101 is just the starting point – the base information that I install in only one practice. My teaching philosophy starts with a simple rule: Build the base, rep it out, and grow. After the base is built with SWAT 101, I rep it out, and expand by teaching the rest of the system in the order shown by subsequent chapters.

SWAT 101 – Day 1

How much more you can do with less is the true measure of a great team.

– SWAT ideology

The Secret

- **WHAT YOU FOCUS ON GROWS.** That's the secret to success by whatever definition is attached to success, in anything you try to accomplish – sports, working out, business, professional career, personal life. Positive or negative, what you devote your attention to is guaranteed to build up. Whatever positive act you devote full attention to will positively grow. Not maybe, not possibly, definitely. But, the same applies to the negative – full attention to the negative positively grows. Full focus is achieved by quality and quantity of extraordinary reps, not just ordinary, average reps. Xs and Os alone will never beat half-assed reps. Xs and Os alone will never substitute mediocre reps. What matters is what you rep-out mentally and physically, and how you rep it out. The type of reps that makes the SWAT system work is the **Power of Infinity**, the kind needed to build **IQ** – **I**nstinct **Q**uotient.

- The **Power of Infinity (∞Reps+ ∞Levels)** is the key to SWAT passing. The actual Xs and Os are secondary. The system's explosiveness is the by-product of the specific type of **focused infinite reps** that lead to continuous growth to infinite next levels of performance. The following is the Power of Infinity theory:

    - ∞**Reps+ ∞Levels.** Performance levels are not limited to rookie and veteran or beginner, intermediate, and expert. Rookies and veterans are not created equal – there are infinite levels of performance. There are infinite performance levels within each general classification of performance. There are infinite steps on the ladder... infinite next-levels. The goal is to reach expertise, upper level performances composed of infinite micro-levels. Experts are not created equal – there are infinite steps on the expert ladder. Infinite reps and infinite performance levels are the secret to the SWAT system.

    - ∞**Reps Rule** – Build the Base, then Grow. Reps are not created equal. Some reps are tougher than others. Our goal is to build the base with same/unchallenging reps, then grow with different/challenging reps. Building the base stabilizes performance, setting the stage for next-level growth.

    - ∞**Reps Rule** applies to every performance level. Every level entered repeats the cycle – build the base, then grow. Every level needs stability with same/unchallenging reps followed by growth reps – different/challenging reps. This cycle governs my practice planning.

    - Quantity and quality of reps separates from the rest – separate from competition, separate from downtime.

    - ∞**Reps+ ∞Levels** is rep-progression that strikes the all-important teaching-learning balance between anxiety and boredom, the real performance killers. It's a solution for dreaded team-killers – complacency and apathy. It solves under-training and over-training.

∞**Reps+** ∞**Levels** is not easy to plan. It is challenging but when you nail it, it works out for player development all the way to expert. It's a guaranteed formula for building strength and skill, and continuously moving toward full potential.

- **BUILD IQ** – Instinct Quotient. Building mental and physical IQ is the secret to winning – automatic, second-nature reps. Football is like any high-risk job – survival depends on speed... high-speed thinking, high-speed doing. A ton of information has to be processed in the blink of an eye and translated into action – power performance. Play-calling, decision-making, and execution in any trenches depends on the power of fully-developed instinct. Not gut feelings, not hunches... instinct – survival-mode instinct. Flipping the switch, calling out the inner force... the inner beast, intellectually and physically, that unleashes hardwired thinking and doing. **Programmed performance.** The highest IQ wins – both on the sidelines and on the field. It's impossible to win with a low IQ. Poor instinct, poor performance. How do you develop high-octane QBs from scratch? Build their IQ with ∞Reps. How do you develop every other position? Same answer. How do you become a master play-caller? Same answer. Football is a problem-solving activity. Coaches and players are problem-solvers. Keeping that in mind solves the mystery to passing, running, throwing, catching, blocking – the mystery of high-speed no-huddle offense.

Base Philosophy

- **Working Out Wins – W.O.W.** ==Championships are won in the weight room.== There is a direct relationship between iron-lifting and championships. Iron efficiency wins championships, iron deficiency doesn't. Xs and Os are meaningless without working out. But, working out is not created equal. Going through the motions doesn't qualify as working out. The quality of a workout is determined by the quantity and quality of reps. Poor conditioning conditions poor results. Our *EXplode* strength training system is more important than any pass play, any running play, any blitz, or any coverage. When my players commit to year-round lifting, we are guaranteed to win. When they don't, we won't.

- **Nothing Just Happens.** Dual-meaning: nothing great just happens automatically; nothing happens at random. You can't just call out the beast on demand. High-level performance doesn't happen overnight. Contrary to popular belief, winners aren't born. They're made. Winners are the product of struggle, not comfort. Winning is the confluence of events, not just a single act. Winning doesn't happen in isolation – winning is connected to a series of negative and positive experiences linked together to form an ironwill mindset.

- **Don't Ignore Simplicity.** Complexities are the product of cluttered minds. Build the basics, stick to the basics. Build automatic, second-nature skills, mentally and physically. Replace thinking with instinct. Simplicity builds instinct, complexity clogs it.

- **Play Your Game, Not Theirs.** Never let the opponent dictate your plan. Proactive leads, reactive follows. Reactive leads to inactivity. No defensive formation, coverage, or blitz ever changes what we do or how we do it. If we have invested enough quality reps into our no-huddle offense, no defensive strategy will stop us. If we invest poorly, any defense will beat us regardless of defensive strategy. We never have followed a defense in three decades and never will.

- **Build the Beast, Call Out the Beast.** Xs and Os are simply an organized way for the beast to release. If the inner beast doesn't release, it's impossible to win. No playbook overcomes a hidden beast. No system beats timidity. Passion or passive – free will. One wins, one loses.

- **Convert the Defensive Pass Rush to the Offensive Pass Rush.** What is focused on is the single-most important element of SWAT passing. Xs and Os will not overcome a QBs fear of the pass rush. Playbooks are useless if the QB focuses on the defensive pass rush. If the QB does not develop an offensive pass rush, the offense will get crushed. Use 3 backs and run the ball.

- **Blitz the Defense — Rush the Defense.** Force the defense to ==Show It and Blow It==. Stay over the speed limit and send out a mob. Commit to 4-5 receivers. And don't blink. Emptying the backfield, empties the defensive tank. Push the defensive fuel needle to E. If you and the QB don't view max receivers as offensive pressure instead of defensive pressure, if you and the QB fear sending out 5 receivers, go to 3-backs and run the ball.

- **BRAVO-ball. Make the Tight End the Feature Back.** The player I used to put at tailback is a now TE, called Bravo. Move him around and throw double-digit passes to him. Force the defense to focus their attention on him. Changing the defense's focus to the TE changes their game – guaranteed. The Bravo-focus builds the strongest bind that we can impose on the defense.

- **The Effects of F/X are Unlimited.** The 4th receiver (X) aligns in the backfield at the conventional fullback position (F). Use a wide receiver or another tight end or conventional fullback. Never align the 4th receiver at his final spot – move him there. F/X is the fullback to X-man transformation on the majority of plays. Next to the focus on Bravo, the F/X move is the most challenging bind we can put a defense in. The combined effects of Bravo-focus and F/X allow us to balance the playing field as over-matched underdogs by building the base for both power-passing and power-running.

- **Win the E Battle – Endurance vs Exhaustion.** Defenses can't play on E. An exhausted defense is an oxymoron. It's not a defense. Football players are not endurance athletes. They are ATP athletes, meaning they can only handle workloads under 10 seconds before needing rest to fill the tank. They can't handle the **pain of lactic acid buildup** that occur when workloads exceed 10 seconds. SWAT turns football into a battle of tanks – empty tanks versus full tanks. Superior strength and fitness always beats talent and skill. Bigger stones beat any Goliath. Nothing intimidates more than a tireless fighter. Nothing instills more fear that fatigue. We changed the term 'strength and conditioning' to 'strength and endurance.' The *EXplode* system specializes in strength and endurance. He who can fight longer wins. Strength and endurance athletes will always win the fight because they can fight longer. Conventional ATP athletes can easily be exhausted. An exhausted defense gets steamrolled.

Playbook: **None. No conventional playbook. A system replaces the playbook that includes three components:**

(i) SWAT dictionary.
(ii) SWAT language.
(iii) SWAT decision-making model – how to make the call.

The SWAT dictionary includes codewords and numbers based on the police communication system that I learned in one day as an 18-year-old rookie cop. The SWAT language is the way we organize the dictionary and communicate plays at the line of scrimmage.

The decision-making model makes the call, deciding what play to build and when. We don't call plays, we build them at the LOS. We build limitless formations through shifts and motion and build running plays or pass plays at the LOS.

The dictionary includes the building blocks. The decision-making model builds the play... makes the call. The decision-making models has 4 components:

(i) decide on run or pass;
(ii) if pass, how to build the plays by combining partial concepts, regardless of what the coverage is;
(iii) how to read coverage and then make the call; and
(iv) how to find open receivers.

I don't teach the QB to read defensive coverage in SWAT 101 because our warp-speed no-huddle forces the defense *to show it and blow it* – when the defense runs out of gas, they become limited, they become predictable, they telegraph their intention, and they mess up alignment and assignment. We have miles/kilometers of video evidence that proves reading defenses is not necessary to pass for 300-600 yards when the no-huddle is speeding far beyond the speed limit. Reading defensive coverages is taught after the base is built in SWAT 101. Coverage recognition is a bonus for the QB, not a necessity. SWAT 101 builds the base, then the system grows after.

Base Strategy

- **8-Second Play-Clock** – 1 play every 8 seconds unravels the defense. Tears them apart. Makes it impossible for the defense to play their intended game. The 8-second play-clock gives the offense **full control** by draining the defense battery, including their sidelines. The 8-second play-clock jams communication between coordinator and field. Unless a defensive player has been trained to call formations, coverages and blitzes, the 8-second clock turns defensive play-calling into a cluster-fuck.

- **Over 80 Rule©** – ==Over 80 plays every game.== More scoring opportunities, more pressure, more game experience to develop players. ==We don't manage the clock, we extend the clock.== We force the defense to play on fumes. No defense we have ever faced has been trained to defend a minimum of 80 offensive plays per game at full speed. They can't and won't. The Over 80 Rule reduces defensive 40-speed. The Over 80 Rule is the only way to turn the slower team into the faster team. That's how a slower team wins the fourth-quarter fight... first in the mind, then in the body.

- **BLITZ the Defense** – Floor it. Pressure the defense with offensive pressure – 4 or 5 receivers has the same effect on defense as defensive blitzes on offense. Maximum receivers lays down the gauntlet – the defense has to make a tough call... drop back or send pressure. Both are wrong when you blitz the defense. Cancel the defensive blitz with an offensive blitz. And if they don't blitz, game's over. Dropping back causes dropping back – on the scoreboard.

- **Stretch the Feature-Back** – In 1985, we kept the feature-back in the backfield. It worked. By 1994, we stretched the feature-back. The feature-back was moved to the #2 receiver online or off-line spot on our right side, appearing to be the Tight End... code-name Bravo. Then, Bravo became the Stretch-Back... we shifted Bravo anywhere horizontally along the LOS, inside or outside the box, online and offline. To achieve our goal of equal ball-distribution, the Bravo TE has a double-digit reception performance demand for every game. Throwing double-digit passes to the Bravo TE has created the strongest defensive bind... our greatest offensive benefit. We don't keep secrets – we tell the defense that we fully intend to pass to Bravo a lot and we challenge them to find him in our formation and cover him... and focus full their full attention on him. If they don't, Bravo will wreck the defense single-handedly. If they do, he will still do damage and so will other receivers who have not been focused on.

- **F/X Shift** – The F/X shift is how we align the 4th receiver. Start the 4th receiver in the backfield and then move him. Stretch the 4th receiver anywhere by aligning him at any spot along the LOS, online, or offline, inside or outside the box. After the defense focuses on Bravo, aligning the 4th receiver in and out of the box builds another coverage bind. The conventional fullback position (Foxtrot) shifts out of the backfield about 95% of plays every game. When he leaves the box he becomes X (X-ray)... the X-man. The shift is call F/X... F becomes X when he shifts outside the box. We use a wide range of personnel at F – wide receiver, tight end, tailback, or, rarely, conventional fullback. The F/X shift creates another powerful defensive bind, both by alignment and assignment. When we leave Foxtrot in the backfield, a stronger bind is built... the 4th receiver aligning in the backfield creates a double-bind after having stretched his alignment along the LOS.

- **Build the Formation** – Shift every play. We build the formation in stages in front of the defense, force a defensive decision and reaction, and evaluate it. Shifting is an offensive advantage and does not compromise our 8-second rule. Not shifting gives the defense an advantage.

- **Limitless Capacity by Connecting Partial Concepts** – Every pass play is a connection of two or more partial concepts. Combined with limitless formations, we build similar images by joining similar concepts from different starting points. Similar images is the key element to raising QB IQ.

- **Build Pass Plays at LOS, Don't Call and Re-Call** –Translate, don't regurgitate.

- **No Reading Defenses Needed Until After We Learn to Play our Game** – Reasons? (i) Reading coverage is not a necessary skill when the no-huddle is operating at warp-speed (ii) time constraints (iii) priority. We've proved that explosive passing is possible and expected without the QB having learning coverage recognition.

- **Post-Snap Detours Alter Pass Routes by Simply Running Away from Defenders in Man or Zone Coverage** – This allows every pass play to be a man-buster or zone-buster. No pass play is the wrong pass play.

- **Pass Plays Start as an OC-QB collaboration Until the QB is Capable of Calling His Own Plays** – If the decision-making models are taught and learned properly, the QB should become, and is expected to become a competent play-caller. QB play-calling dramatically increases no-huddle speed and efficiency. There's a direct relationship between the QB calling his own plays and the percentage of completed passes, number of long-distance plays, and points scored.

- **OC uses the SCORES Decision-Making Model©** to make the call – run or pass.

- **OC calls the temporary formation** and the shifts/motions to build the final formation.

- **OC starts the pass play** by calling the front-side partial concept.

- **QB finishes the play by calling backside concept**... until he takes over play-calling. QB performance rose by a minimum 300% when they started participating in pass-play construction at the LOS. You understand what you help build. QBs found receivers easier because they knew where everyone would be by understanding the play as opposed to memorizing and recalling hundreds of diagrams. Every pass play is a connection of two partial concepts – two pieces that the QB can understand how they fit together. But our QB performance skyrockets when they take over play-calling. My evidence shows a direct relationship between QB performance and QB control of play-calling. Every one of our QBs who has progressed to 100% play-calling control has dominated by shattering league records. QBs who mastered the 50% pass-play-building became league all-stars. But QBs who had zero control of play-calling in our old system struggled – underachievers. The turning point in QB performance was when I scrapped conventional pass plays in a conventional playbook. The OC-QB pass-play building partnership raised the passing bar beyond my expectations.

- Both the OC and QB use the 5-S decision-making model to build pass plays at the LOS, and without reading defensive coverage.

- After QB masters the 5-S model, the SCORES decision-making model is taught to the QB so he can make all play-calls himself. SCORES teaches pre-snap defensive formation and coverage recognition to determine whether run or pass is called, and which type of specific run or pass. No audibles are needed. SCORES eliminates the need for change of play.

- The QB uses the BOARD THEORY to find open receivers, replacing read progressions. Instead of conventional post-snap read progression, QB **sees the board** and makes the call regarding whom to throw to.

- Teach pass system first, run system second. Reasons: (i) what you focus on grows (ii) concept of 'included reps' – running plays are included in passing reps, not vice-versa.

Theory

- **Never Make the Mistake of Presumption of Perfect Coverage** – The **presumption of perfect coverage** is the single-greatest limitation that inhibits passing. The presumption of perfect coverage is the belief that a defense's called coverage will work exactly as planned and diagrammed. Instant credibility and automatic assumption that whatever coverage is called will work perfectly. Every time you teach that a pass play will not work against a certain coverage, you have made the **mistake of presumption of perfect coverage**. You have taught the offense to wrongly believe that whatever coverage the defense called will be perfectly executed and will positively work by fully covering all receivers. It won't. No coverage will be perfectly executed. It's not possible. I learned this fact as defensive coordinator. It took me until 1994 to break my worst coaching habit that was holding back the full force of our passing system – my habit of teaching, warning, scaring our offense that specific pass plays would not work against specific coverages... that pass plays had to match coverages – the habit of presuming perfect coverage. When I realized how difficult coverage is to teach, learn, and master, I kicked the habit. I stopped letting coverage dictate play calling. In two magical seasons, 1994 and 1995, we built up enough evidence that proved if partial passing concepts are properly connected, receivers make the right detours and the no-huddle breaks speed limits, any pass play will work against any coverage – guaranteed.

- **Full-Force, Full-Impact** – Maximum pressure unravels any defense. Defenses are guaranteed to crack under intense pressure. We define offensive pressure as **full-force** – forcing the defense to play faster, think faster, and cover all 5 receivers every play. Full-force is the best way to make full-impact with mismatched players. We don't know how to pass with low-force or low-impact. We never practice sending only 2 or 3 receivers. Zero reps. We don't train with low force. We train only at full-throttle. We have a broken switch – once it's on, it stays on. Fight like you train, train like you fight. It's the DNA and personality of our offense. You can't genetically modify your offensive DNA. We train with the full-force of 4-5 receivers and play the same way. Power passing and power running by breaking defensive will. I have never used the phrase "*smash mouth*" and never will for legal purposes – to prevent civil liability. Instead, I teach full-force, high-impact passing and running achieved by flipping the switch, draining the opponent's strength, and steamrolling the defense.

- **Addition by Subtraction** – Defenses can only handle natural pressure, that which they have been trained to handle. Adding unnatural pressure shrinks the defensive playbook. Unnatural pressure thrown at the defense reduces defensive mental and physical recovery time and reduces decision-making time. Defenses become predictable and limited while offense becomes unlimited. **The need to read defenses is diminished.**

- **Pre-Exhaustion** – Offensive Pressure that neutralizes and exceeds defensive pressure is achieved by **relentless challenges** – limitless formations, limitless pass plays, power passing, and power running. Force the defense to cover every inch of the field and every receiver, on every play.

    Maximum spread: land and people. Inclusive ball distribution – throw everywhere and to every receiver… include everyone and every place. **No breaks until they break.** My film study shows one consistent piece of evidence – **every defense has a break point, no matter how much more talented they are than you. Their break point is the point where you give them no break.** Instead of trying to match Xs and Os, match will. Make football into a battle of will by flooring the gas pedal. Iron-will wins. I have witnessed the X Factor repeatedly, the secret to winning – *pre-exhaustion*. Pre-exhaustion is the false message that the mind sends when the bar is raised and the pain of hard work goes past the natural threshold, the line that separates what you're used to and what you're not used to. Pre-exhaustion is the mind bullshitting the body, telling it to quit because the workload has entered uncharted territory. When you bring the opponent to a place they are unwilling and incapable of handling, you win. Guaranteed. Pre-exhaustion is the X Factor of the SWAT system. It's the secret that leads to unrivaled performances with inferior talent. I have seen it in the gym, I've seen in on the field, I've seen it in the trenches of real-life… the mind cannot handle a prolonged fight that it has not trained for. The mind can't flip the switch on demand. It cannot handle unnatural exertion. You can't call out the inner beast on demand. I have seen people give up because of intense fear brought on by the mere thought of manual labour. I have seen people give up far before the tank is empty simply because of weak minds – soft, mushy minds. Especially the artificial steroid-induced bodies. I teach my players that anabolic-agent addicts are the easiest to beat. Don't fear their appearance. Steroid addicts are weak people who cannot handle the rigors of the natural struggle. That's why they by-pass it with performance-enhancing drugs. You can learn to outwork anyone, including the genetically-gifted. Some may be blessed with DNA-force but no one is born with guts. Balls are developed. It starts at the top – mindset. To compete against stronger competition, weaken them… with SWAT – secret weapon attitude training. Pre-exhaustion is the strongest offensive strategy we have in our system because it attacks the softest part of any opponent – their minds.

- **Never Ignore Simplicity** – A limitless system does not complicate for the sake of bragging that our playbook is bigger than yours. Studying our offense's film makes it seem that we have a huge playbook but we don't. We simply change appearance without changing the system. Change without change. Our system is the equivalent of running similar races with different starting blocks. Limitless formations are built with SWAT Language starting with a temporary formation and shift/motions to the final formation simply takes advantage of offensive rules. Forcing the defense to re-align disrupts defensive play-calling and reveals their intention. Defenses will show it and blow it. Any time you force any one to adjust to anything, you increase the chances of a breakdown.

- **Psychology is Far More Important Than Straight Xs and Os** – No properly 5S constructed pass play is the wrong call. Every route is intended to go deep. Short-distance or long-distance passes are all intended to go deep. Blocking after the catch is the key. And going deep inside every offensive player is more important than a player's current skill level. The willingness and capacity to go deep is the difference between winning and losing. It's fashionable for players to trash-talk and mouth-off about how tough they are simply because they play football but the reality is this – no one is born with the will to go deep on every play. And they won't. Human nature opposes going deep. Never presume that an opponent has ironwill. Ordinary toughness is not ironwill. Ordinary toughness has limits. Ironwill is a special quality that is not common, not even in the mythical world of football. We all want to believe that ironwill is inherent to football but it's not. Ironwill is an unbreakable mindset, a force that will not cave into any adversity, but it simply will not just happen. It takes extreme work to build. Enormous investment. In my experience, the majority will not invest the right amount. Build iron-will first, then worry about technique, and Xs and Os.

- **Deep Force** – Think of how hard it is to make players buy-in to wind sprints. We send receivers deep almost every play, running plays included. Why? Knock-out punch. Going deep is both a force and a threat. The threat of going deep on every play is a force stronger than actually going deep. How do you strengthen a running game versus Goliath? Threaten to go deep on every play. Force defenders to run a lot. Nothing beats Goliath than forcing him to run. Running is the soft spot of every defense, bar none. Sprinting is the equivalent of body shots that soften a fighter right before the KO punch.

- **The Myth of Finesse Teams** – Bullshit baffles brains. Every time I hear self-professed experts ramble about finesse teams, I'm reminded of the 66% conformity rule – a minimum of two-thirds of humans will believe any bullshit even if the bullshit contradicts logic and personal beliefs.[3] In other words, more people are followers than leaders. We have provided overwhelming evidence to prove that the *'finesse'* label is nonsensical and foolish. It's just another example of labeling something simply because you don't understand it or can't do it yourself because it's too hard to do or you can't stop it or beat it. Our POWER PASSING is exactly the same as our POWER RUNNING – it will ground and pound you. Full-impact passing is the equivalent of a one-sided street-fight where a lightweight throws bomb after bomb at lightning speed on a heavyweight who rarely sees one. We're not a *finesse* team, we're a *fitness* team. When all our cylinders are firing, we have upset every Goliath that we have willing moved up to face, not by finesse, but by muscling them. Contrary to popular myth, pass blocking is not passive blocking. Pass blocking is more aggressive, more demanding, and more challenging than run blocking. Our downfield blockers after a catch are just as aggressive as any run blocker. I mold our offense the same way I have molded defenses – **mobile, agile, hostile**... the secret to power-playing.

---

[3] Tribute to masterpieces – conformity research by Milgram, Zimbardo, and Asch. Their studies showed that a minimum of 66% will be conform to the thoughts and behaviours of others even if it conflicts with their self-belief. There are positives and negatives to this force of human nature. On the positive side, effective leadership easily achieves buy-in of a message that the leader tries to get across. On the negative side, the majority of people don't have a mind of their own and can be easily swayed for nefarious purposes. Refer to bibliography

Teaching Strategy

- I use the Base Play (Stretch Pass) as the point-of-reference to teach the SWAT dictionary, language, and decision-making model.

- The Stretch Pass is the context to which all the components of the system attach to.

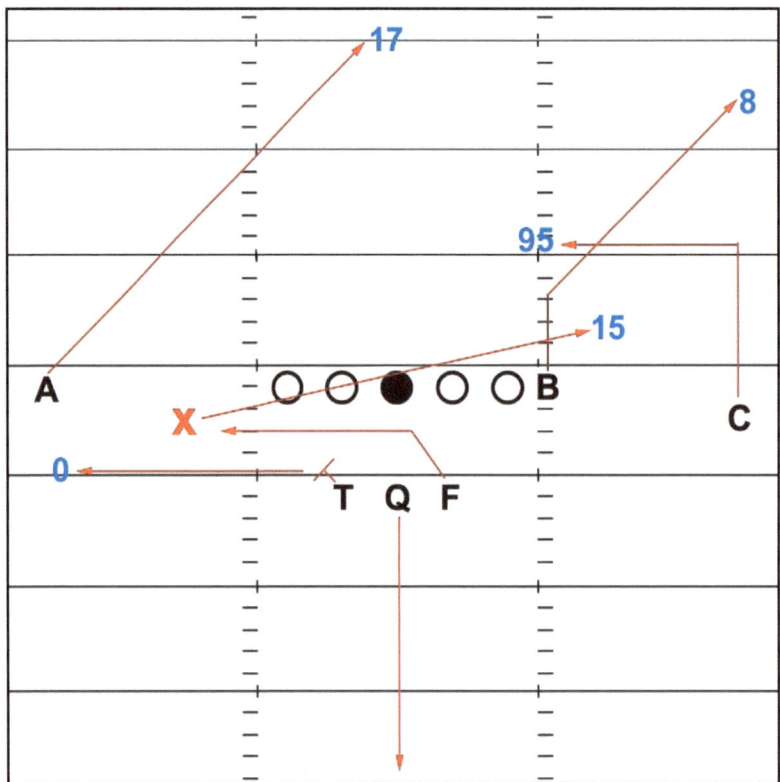

Elements of the Stretch Pass

- **Stretch vertically, stretch horizontally, fill the gap (in the middle).** Two stretches – deep and wide then fill the hole in between.

- **Frontside** — corner-in partial concept. In SWAT language: "*Bravo Charlie 8-95*" meaning **Bravo** runs 8 pattern (3-step vertical + 45-degrees to the corner); **Charlie** runs a 95 pattern (6-step vertical = 90-degree in).

- **Backside** — high-low cross (aka double-cross) partial concept. In SWAT language: "*Alpha X-Ray 17-15*" meaning **Alpha** runs 17 (no-vertical 75-degree post); **X-Ray** runs a 15 pattern (no-vertical 30-degree low cross). "*Tango Zero*" meaning **Tailback** looks in, out and releases to flare route behind LOS, parallel to his alignment.

- **F/X shift** — in SWAT language: "*Mike 2*" meaning **FB** moves to 2 spot (inside slot receiver on left side) and becomes "**X**".

- **Starting formation** — "*Quick Gun Bravo 4*" meaning **Quick Gun** (2-back shotgun); "*Bravo 4*" aligns **TE** online at 4 spot (right-side).

- **41 FS/BS ratio** — 4 receivers in frontside; 1 backside. The two partial concepts connect, merging to form a 4-receiver frontside. This forms a 4-piece **board**, referring to 3 receivers in the same sight line and a 4th in the same vision area, and 4 equally-spaced vertically, horizontally and at 3 levels – deep, middle, short.

- **4 total levels of receivers** — including the tailback, the receivers are positioned at 4 levels deep, middle, short, behind LOS.

- **2 FS directions** — 3 to sideline, 1 away from sideline.

- **Triple-receivers in same sight-line** — 3 receivers in single sight-line.

- **2 hot receivers** — tailback and X-ray.

- **46/55 security protection** — 4 or 5 receivers release, 5 or 6 blockers.

- **33 protection** — 3 right, 2 left, 1 back left (search protector) – 4 big on big.

- **Cadence** — three plays called, first play live, snap on first sound.

- **Limitless formations** — the combined effect of two backfield formations + 16 online/offline receiver spots + SWAT language builds limitless formations at the LOS without a playbook and without memorizing hundreds of formation diagrams.

- **SWAT language** — the stretch play diagram shows the starting formation Quick Gun Bravo 4. That phrase aligns the entire offense – 2-back shotgun backfield, Alpha and Bravo receivers on-line at the wide(1) and tight(4) spots respectively, Charlie receiver aligns offline at the right wide spot (6). The SWAT formation language and the shift/motion language has limitless capacity – limitless formations.

- **Same snap count** — first sound.

- **Read progression** — not the conventional high-low-check down. No primary receiver. No progression of 1st to 4th receiver. Instead:

    i. see the whole board

    ii. know the situation

    iii. make the call

    iv. remember it

Every player receiver and back has a codename from the police phonetic alphabet: Alpha, Bravo, Charlie, Tango, Foxtrot (X-Ray is the 4th receiver – Foxtrot is the first motion man who becomes X when he shifts).

- **Base pass routes** — 10 single-digit numbers – odd to QB, even to sideline.

- **Limitless pass routes** — by combining base routes – 2 or 3 digit pass routes.

- **Pass play call** — receiver code names + corresponding routes (ie: Bravo Charlie 8-95).

- **Running play call** — three-digit number ie: 367 - Ball-carrier, intended point-of-attack, blocking scheme respectively.

- Formation Calls
    - only 2 temporary backfield formations: I, shotgun (called Quick Gun);
    - three online alignments;
    - limitless final formations by shifting Foxtrot and/or Tango to receiver, or offline receivers anywhere horizontally by a simple phonetic code-word and number.

Shift/Motion – Use a phonetic code-word to instruct a back or WR to move to a single or double-digit number that designates an offline alignment along LOS.

5-S QB Decision-Making Model© to Call pass play:

   1 -   Separate receivers from each other

   2 -   Separate receivers from defenders

   3 -   Same sight-line (max receivers in on vision line)

   4 -   Steer safeties

   5 -   Safety valve – one hot receiver minimum.

Procedure

- One huddle at beginning of every drive. QB instructs: "number of plays called, which one is live, snap count." In SWAT 101: *"3 plays called, 1st live, first sound... got it – BREAK."*
- AT LOS:

(i) OC calls "*QUICK GUN BRAVO 4*" (temporary/1st/starting alignment).

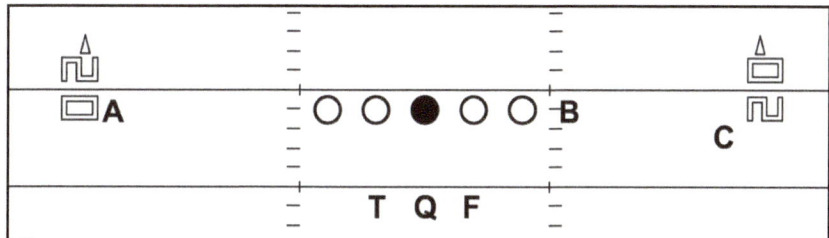

Foxtrot is not exclusively a conventional fullback. He is either:

(a) another Bravo receiver (Big End – BE), a strong-safety type of player capable of playing X or Y in the limitless SWAT Defense, or

(b) a wide receiver who can play defense as a DB, or

(c) a conventional FB.

There are only 2 SWAT backfield formations: 2-back I, 2-back Shotgun. Motion/shifts are used to build limitless formations. The shotgun formation features a formation bind:

(a) 2 Big Ends on the same side, one in the backfield (Foxtrot) who re-aligns at one of 16 numbered spots online or offline, or

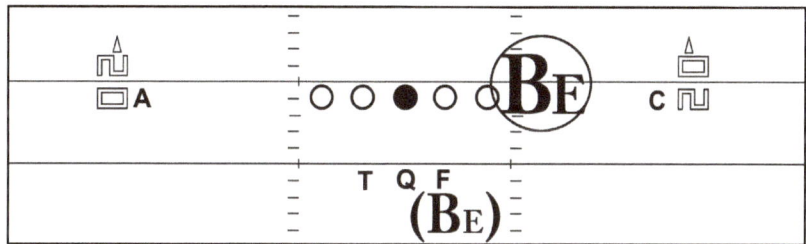

(b) 2 WRs on an unconventional trips side, 1 WR in the backfield forces the defense to declare how they will cover #3 (foxtrot) in our starting formation.

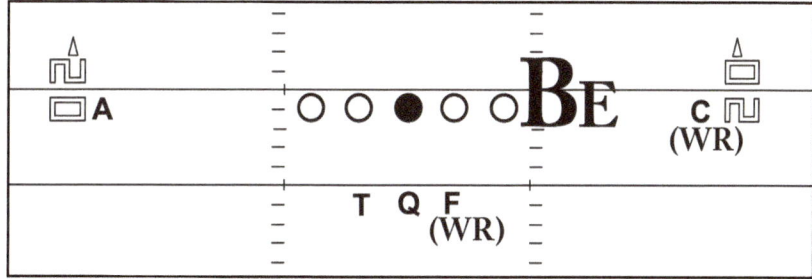

This diverse personnel grouping triples the number of Stretch Pass Plays – 3 in 1. Three plays per each play.

(ii) OC calls shift: **"Mike 2"** (Foxtrot moves to 2 spot and becomes X in a 2x2 single-back shotgun).

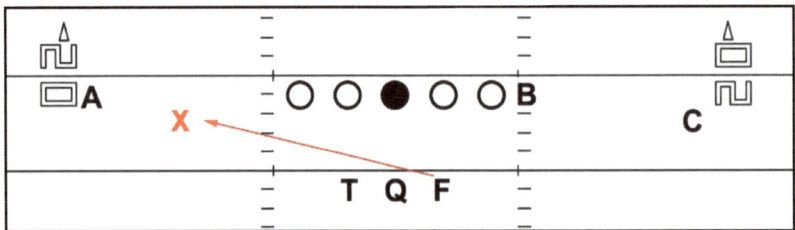

(iii) OC signals FS by calling a partial concept – **"Bravo Charlie 8-95"** (corner-in)

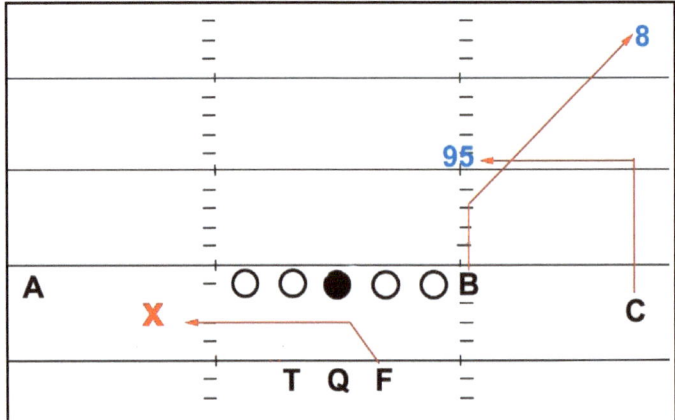

(iv) QB uses the 5-S decision-making model to finish play by calling BS partial concept using pattern digits only from left to right into the backfield – **"17, 15, zero"** meaning: High-Low Cross with TB look in, out and release to flare.

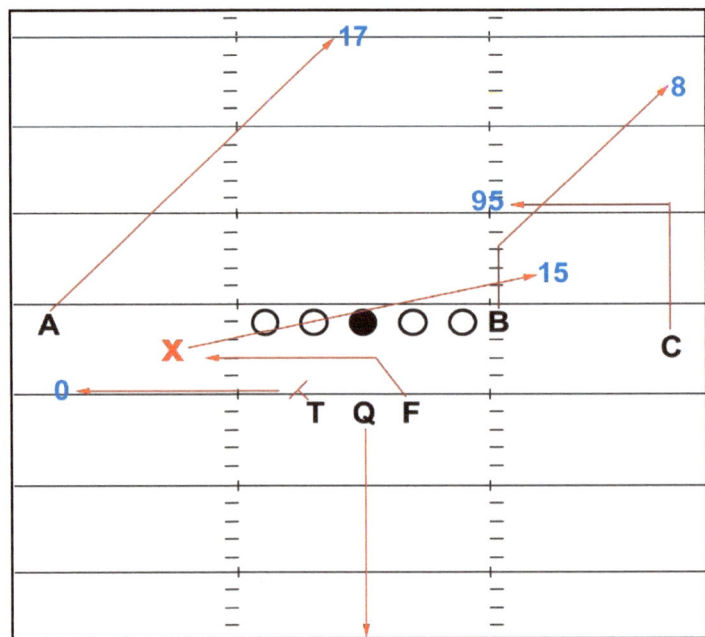

(v)   2 dummy calls: ie: 367, 208 (both are running plays).

(vi) First word, ball is snapped (ie: Down, ready, set, go, hut... any of these words).

(vii) QB drops 5-steps.

(viii) QB stares at deep middle for 3-steps.

(ix) QB search FS (front-side) – move eyes to 45 degrees. See the whole board, know the situation, make the call (find open man), remember it (burn the image into memory). Each route is intended to go deep. Shorter passes have the advantage of more downfield blockers. The 95-in pattern has two lead blockers. The 15-low cross has three blockers with structured blocking assignments.

(x)   QB as a ball-carrier. QBs are not taught to scramble. We teach them to run. There's a difference. Converting a stretch pass to a running play needs organized blocking, decision-making, and simulated practice.

Summary of Procedures

- Huddle once at beginning of every drive
- QB calls number of total plays called, which on is live, and snap count
- En route to LOS, OC calls staring formation

In the above example, 3 total plays are called, the first play is live, the 2nd and 3rd are dummy calls. The QB pauses after the third play and the ball is snapped on the QB's first sound, after the pause, on one of five words: GO, DOWN, READY, SET, HUT.

The result is a 46 pass play – 4 receivers + 6 blockers that can change into 55 (5 receivers + 5 blockers) if 6 defenders don't rush. This procedure has limitless capacity. Limitless formation, limitless pass plays, limitless concepts.

The pass play connects 2 partial concepts to form a full concept:

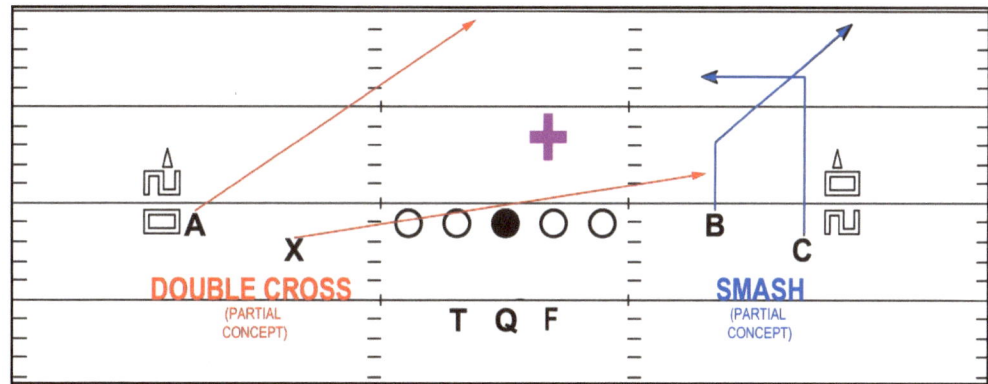

Two receivers stretch deep coverage toward the opponent's goal line. One receiver stretches short coverage toward the LOS. The fourth splits the middle. The result is stretch and split.

The corner pattern stretches 2 ways – goal line and sideline. Two horizontal stretches spread toward the sidelines, short and deep. Two vertical stretches spread toward the goaline. Another horizontal stretch happens on the middle seam. Stretch and Split. It works against any coverage. The play stretches both man and zone coverage. Stretch and Split is both a man-buster and zone-buster.

Downtime Theory

The offense controls the defense by cutting down downtime: ==downtime is the time between downs.== The 40-second clock is an advantage for the defense. It allows defensive recovery time, decision-making time, and communication time.

The first play after the huddle that opens the drive is the only play in the drive where the speed of scrimmage-setup is not an issue. The time needed for the official to place the ball and setup a line of scrimmage is fixed on the first play – it can't be accelerated.

But, scrimmage-setup for every play afterward plays a major factor in SWAT strategy. Every play, pass or run requires work – energy expenditure during the play. Energy expenditure is forgotten after the play, during the setup time between plays... the unit-formation time.

Conventional huddles minimize the mental and physical energy expended to setup the line-of-scrimmage and offense and defensive formation. The key to the SWAT No-Huddle is to change the downtime by forcing the defense to work hard after the play, during the setup time. No downtime — No downtime between downs. Reduction of downtime completely changes the defense. There's a direct relationship between downtime and defensive performance. Diminished downtime diminishes defensive performance. Defenses are creatures of habit. They are conditioned to function with downtime. Downtime is their comfort zone. Warp-speed no-huddle takes defenses out of their comfort zone into a discomfort zone that slows down their pass rush, coverage, and pursuit. And it eliminates their recovery time, decision-making time, and communication time which shrinks their playbook. The offense controls the defense by cutting down downtime.

Reading Coverages

The reduction of downtime makes it unnecessary for QBs to learn how to read coverage while they are learning the SWAT system. Coverage recognition is taught after QBs master the system. Three reasons:

(i) Point-zero QBs can only learn one thing at a time. Coverage recognition is a complex learning unit that will interfere with learning the SWAT system. It's impossible for QBs to simultaneously learn the SWAT system and reading defenses.

(ii) Coverage becomes predictable against high-speed no-huddle.

(iii) Our QBs have excelled without having mastered coverage recognition.

Our teaching progression starts with learning the SWAT system first. Reading defenses is never taught until the QB has mastered the system. System mastery is defined as:

(a) winning, and

(b) minimum 300-yard single-game passing performance.

SCORES

This is a decision-making model I designed that teaches how to read defenses and make the right corresponding call. It is not taught in SWAT 101 for the reasons mentioned above.

Benefits of the Stretch Pass

- **Beats any coverage** — if the QB is protected, no coverage will shut down the Stretch Pass completely. As long as the QB is standing, the Stretch Pass can beat any coverage. The Stretch Pass includes both zone-buster and man-buster elements by stretching the defense vertically and horizontally creating a void in the middle that gets filled with a receiver sprinting toward the QB. And receivers make structured detour decisions to find open area.

- **Versus Cover Zero** — guaranteed touchdown. The no-vertical release post cannot and the corner pattern will never be 100% covered on the same play. The low-cross is never 100% covered versus any type of man coverage because:

(i) it's the equivalent of a horizontal fly pattern

(ii) the slant release prevents bump disruption

(iii) using a WR in the backfield who shifts to #2 guarantees a mismatch.

The in-pattern breaks at 90-degrees. Separation is simple. If 6 rush, 6 block. The stretch pass guarantees huge running lanes for the QB.

- **Versus Cover 1** — the free safety is put in a bind, cover the post or cover the corner. Either way, he's wrong.

- **Versus Cover 2 Man** — the in-route, low-cross and the TB release will never both be 100% covered.

- **Versus Any Type of Zone** — two high-low binds are created:

(i) the in-and-low cross, and

(ii) the corner and the in.

And the two deep patterns adjust to sprint the seam. The two deep-post and corner routes routinely beat 2 and 3 deep zone coverages. Never give the presumption of perfect coverage.

- 100% of the receivers have never been 100% covered. The only person who stops the stretch play is the QB by:

(i) not finding an open receiver;

(ii) not throwing an accurate pass;

(iii) not negating pressure by hitting the hot receivers. There are 3 potential hot receivers – Alpha, X-Ray and Tango. Any slant release is a hot pattern; or

(iv) not finding a running lane and running.

- Our QBs are ball-carriers — they are not coddled. All our QBs pressure the defense by being dual- threats. SWAT QBs are trained to be mobile, agile, and hostile. We never have had a weak-minded, weak-willed QB and never will.

- Every route is intended to go deep, either by long pass or by run after catch. There is no such thing as a short pattern in the SWAT system.

SWAT Psychology – Secret Weapon Altering Talent

- **DARE to Pass.** Distance After Reception Explodes. ==There are only two ways to win in football: (i) recruit natural talent and let them play at full-strength, or (ii) recruit the outcasts and weaken natural talent. Those are the only two ways – recruit the best or build the best by passing by the best.==

    Yards-After-the-Catch (YAC) is the most powerful force guaranteed to weaken a Goliath defense. YAC changes the game. The distance traveled after a catch debilitates the defense mentally and physically. It drains them. Negative transformation. No offensive play demoralizes a defense like consistent yards after catch. No offensive strategy can gain more yards in faster time. YAC is the supersonic way to travel when your offense is outmatched. Distance after reception explodes the game and the defense by being **SWAT** – Secret Weapon Altering Talent. YAC changes natural talent to ordinary talent. Long distances gained after the catch is the way to genetically modify the DNA of the genetically-gifted. The only reason that natural talent wins is that it's allowed to play at full- strength. If you're like us and have to play against greater natural talent every week, remember the #1 rule – never play them at full-strength. Don't let natural talent run on a full tank.

    A pass is nothing more than a longer QB-ballcarrier exchange... a longer handoff. The catch is equivalent of the starting point of a running play, downfield. Change the focus, change the outcome. Focus on YAC and DARE. Game after game, when the explosion happens we win. When we don't DARE, we lose.

    How do you increase YAC? ∞ Reps. Live reps. Make performance demands of running long distances after every catch in practice. We've done that for decades. If that seems like too much running... quit. Leave the team before you quit during the game.

- **Pressure Breaks You... or Makes You.** A protected QB guarantees DARE. QB protection starts in the gym. Iron efficiency builds iron will. No-Huddle pass blocking is not the same as conventional pass blocking. No-Huddle pass blocking is the equivalent of Over 80 street-brawls in succession. Our blockers have to protect the QB up to 50 times per game and then run block... literally. Our linemen have to be athletes to execute about a dozen counter-gaps. The job qualification of our blockers is simple – mobile, agile, hostile. Just like our QB, receivers and running backs. The place where it's built is the weight room. That's where our natural talent is built. I have worked out for 42 years naturally... no steroids, no performance-enhancing drugs. And the same is expected from every player who goes through our program. No exceptions. Drug Free. Clean is the only option. Steroids is the coward's way out to circumvent the natural struggle which is the whole point of sports – teaching, learning, experiencing, and feeling the natural struggle. That's the biggest life lesson that we teach. I don't have a conventional 'don't-do-drugs' message. Mine is more powerful. It's about the last death I investigated as a detective. The whole speech is in my new book *Soul of a Lifter*.

    The other life lesson I teach is ==not to fear being different – don't fear risk, don't fear challenging conventional wisdom...== because that's the key to real-life survival and success. I teach these lessons with my no-kicking policy. Go for it on every 4th down anywhere on the field – no exceptions. Go for 2-points after every TD – no exceptions. Onside kick 50% of kickoffs. Trust your offense and trust your defense. But most importantly, learn to back it up. He who asserts must prove. Build up the evidence that unconventional thinking works.

Chapter 2: SWAT Dictionary and Language
10 Elements

The SWAT dictionary is composed of a language based on the police communication system. Composed of words and numbers, it uses the phonetic alphabet, 10-code, and 900-code numbering system. The language communicates wide-ranging full or partial sentences that are easily translated at the LOS. Limitless strategies can be designed using this language.

The SWAT dictionary has 10 Elements that form a paperless no-playbook system:

1. Receiver code names.
2. Backfield code names and numbers.
3. 2 backfield formations.
4. Online/offline formations: receiver alignment/positions.
5. Starting-point formation call.
6. Motion/shift code names.
7. Building the final formation (do sequence chart).
8. Pass routes.
9. Hole numbers – intended points of running attack (IPOA).
10. Run blocking concepts/rules.

ELEMENTS 1, 2 and 3

These first 3 elements interact:

1. Receiver code names.

Player	Code Name	Position
A	Alpha	Left wide receiver (#1 left)
B	Bravo	Right inside receiver (#2 right)
C	Charlie	Right outside receiver (#1 right)
X	X-Ray	4th receiver – when F shifts/motions outside the box, F becomes X

2. Backfield code names and numbers.

Q	Quebec	Quarterback
F	Foxtrot	Fullback
T	Tango	Tailback

3. Backfield formations.

- Backfield formations are half of the formation call, not the entire formation call. The receiver online/offline alignments constitute the second half of the formation call.
- I and Quick Gun are temporary formations – starting points.
- Shifts/motion change the temporary formation into any one of limitless formations.
- The fullback shifts/motions to create limitless single-back final formations.
- Both backs may shift/motion to create limitless empty-backfield formations.
- All receivers are identified by a code name (using the police phonetic alphabet).
- All backfield players are identified by both a phonetic alphabet code name and a single digit.

Quick Gun Formation

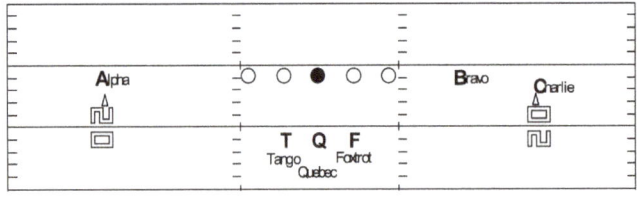

I Formation

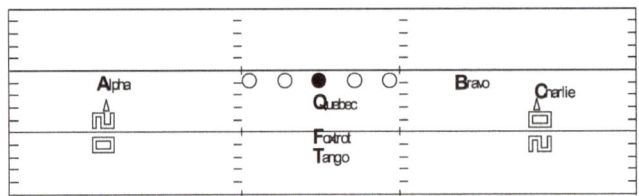

ELEMENT 4

Online/Offline Formations: Receiver Alignment/Positions
- A total of 16 receiver spots have been designated to build unlimited formations.
- All 16 are identified numerically.
- Eight are identified by single digits.
- Eight are identified by double digits.
- All 16 may be online or offline formations.

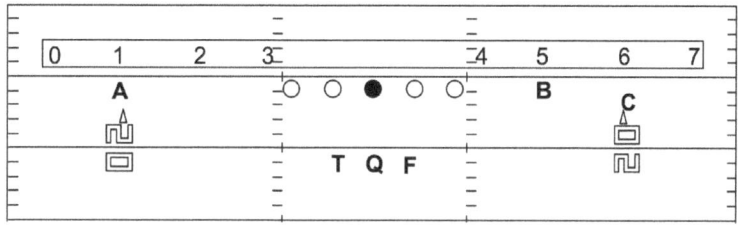

Single Digit – each single digit has an alignment name:

LEFT	RIGHT
1 – Stretch	4 – Inside Tight
2 – Base Wide	5 – Flex (Slot)
3 – Flex (Slot)	6 – Base Wide
	7 – Stretch

- 1 and 6 = conventional "base" spots for wide receivers (online or offline).
- Inside numbers = ball in the middle.
- Outside numbers = ball on hash.
- 3 and 4 = tight/inside receiver spots – tight ends (online) or inside receivers (1X1 offline).
- 0 and 7 = "stretch" spots, half the distance between base/wide and sidelines (stretching the formation to its maximum).
- 2 and 5 = flex/slot spots, half the distance between the base/wide and inside/tight.

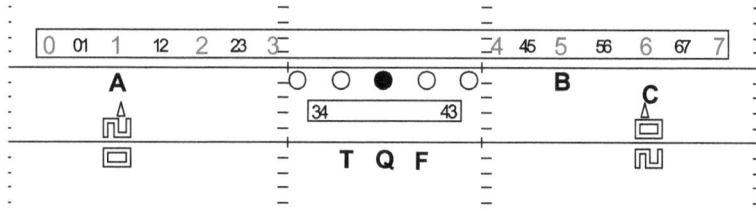

Double digit positions are used to cluster receivers close together:
- 01, 12, 23 are mid-points on the left side.
- 45, 56, 67 are mid-points on the right side.
- All double digit positions are outside the box except for two:
  » 34 and 43 – These two are offset RB alignments inside the box, in B gap – the midpoint between the guard and tackle.

ELEMENT 5

Starting-Point Formation Call

The initial formation has a 2-part name:

    i) Backfield

    ii) Online/offline receiver alignment = Receiver Groups (*example*):

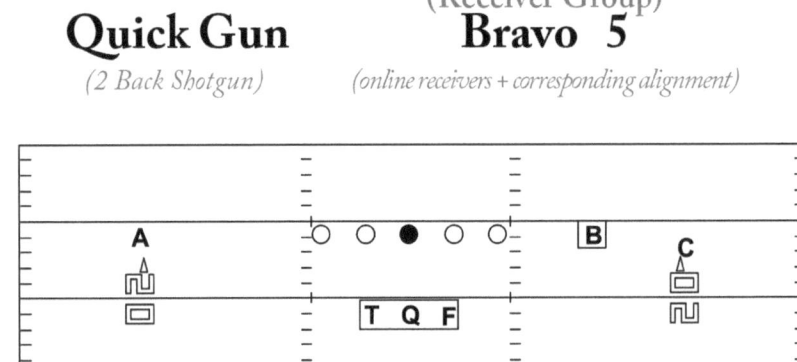

Backfield   +   Receivers' alignment (Receiver Group)

Quick Gun   **Bravo 5**

(2 Back Shotgun)   *(online receivers + corresponding alignment)*

Key Points:

- Quick Gun = Shotgun (both backs = nose in B gap).
- Bravo aligns online at "5" (flex/slot).
- Alpha automatically aligns online at position "1".
- Charlie automatically aligns offline at position "6".
    - » Quick gun aligns 3 players (QB, TB, FB).
    - » Bravo 5 aigns 3 receivers (A, B, C).

There are only 3 receiver alignment groups:

    i) Bravo (plus number) — Alpha and Bravo online, by 7-man LOS rule;

    ii) AC (plus number) — Alpha and Charlie online; and

    iii) XB (plus number) — X-Ray and Bravo online.

    The changing numbers after Bravo, AC or XB provide limitless formation capacity.

ELEMENT 6

Motion/Shift Code Names

Re-alignment of receivers occurs by calling one of four code names plus an alignment/position number. Example: Lima 2. Lima identifies who re-aligns and the direction – the "number" designates the "re-alignment position."

Four code names (words) communicate motion/shift:

OscaR - means "offline left WR motions/shifts Right"

Lima - means "offline right WR motions/shifts Left"

Mike - means "FB motions/shifts" (Mike means Midline player)

DeLTA - means "TB motions/shifts" (DeLTA means Left TailBack)

Example #1: Quick Gun Bravo 4, lima 2

- Charlie is the right offline receiver who shifts/motions left to the 2 spot.

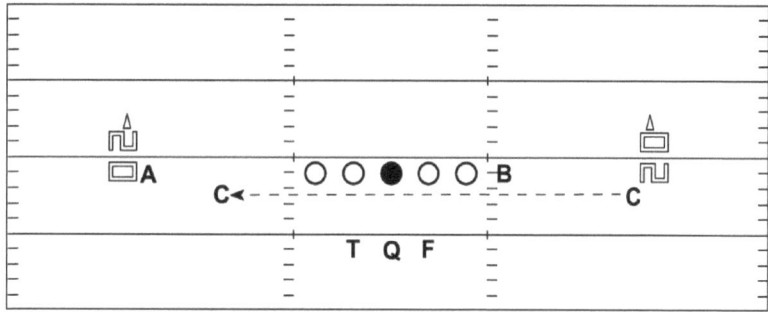

Example #2: Quick Gun AC, Lima 2

- Bravo is the right offline receiver who shifts/motions left to the 2 spot.

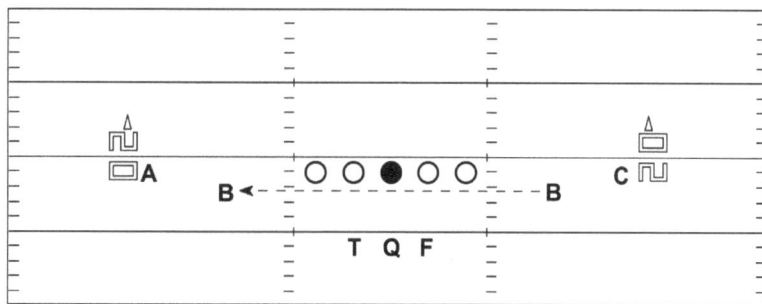

ELEMENT 7

Building The Final Formation

The final formation is called in stages by applying elements #5 and #6.

Example: Transition from base to shotgun/empty formation

Step #1 Temporary formation is called:

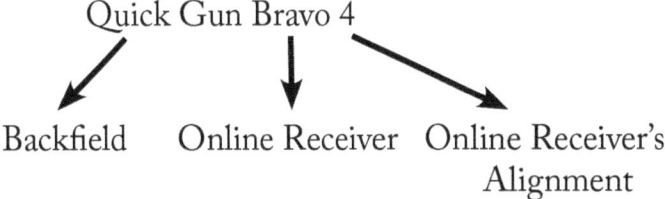

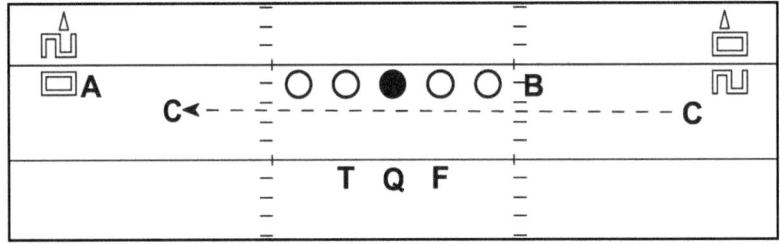

Step #2 First re-alignment: Lima 2 (Charlie motions/shifts Left to 2 spot.)

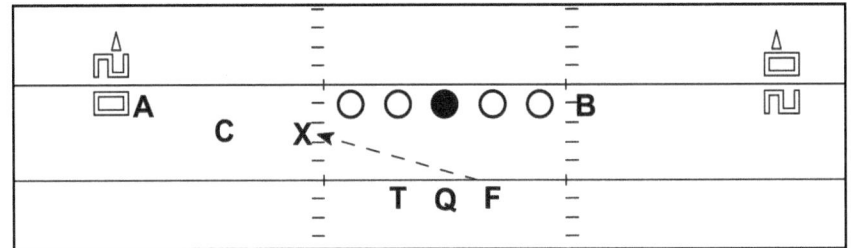

Step #3 Second re-alignment: Mike 3 (FB motions/shifts to 3 spot.)

Note: "FX" concept – F converts to X once outside the box (see element #1 above)."

Step #4 Third re-alignment: Delta 45 (TB motions/shifts to 45 spot.)

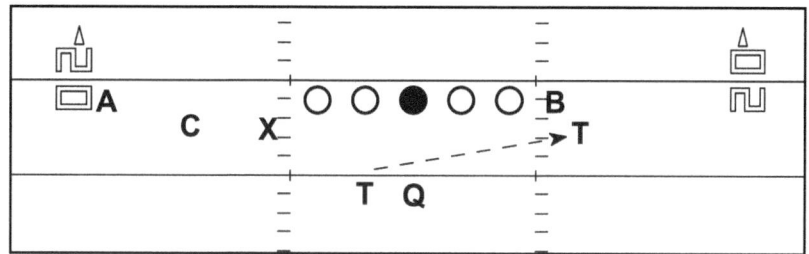

Final Formation

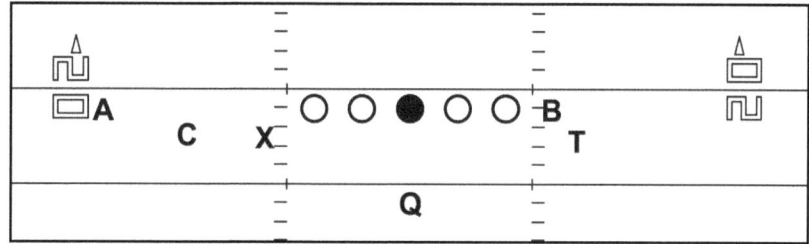

Key Points

- Shotgun empty 3x2.
- No memorization of formation.
- Players translate instead of memorizing.
- The process of changing from 2 backs to empty takes approximately 3 seconds.
- QB and OC can observe the defensive response to make informed decisions.

ELEMENT 8

Pass Routes

The SWAT pass route system has limitless capacity. A simple numbering system can build a limitless tree of pass patterns. The pass route system has 4 pass route trees: Short, Long, Combo/Unlimited, and RB routes.

The first two are base receiver trees. The third is a limitless trees that combines the first two. The fourth is a backfield tree that can build by combining routes.

Short Tree

- 10 routes
- 0 – 9
- odd to ball
- even to sidelines
- 3-step vertical release

We count steps, not yards. It's proven to be the best way to accomplish 2 things:

i) Receivers pattern efficiency, and

ii) Matching pattern with QB's drop.

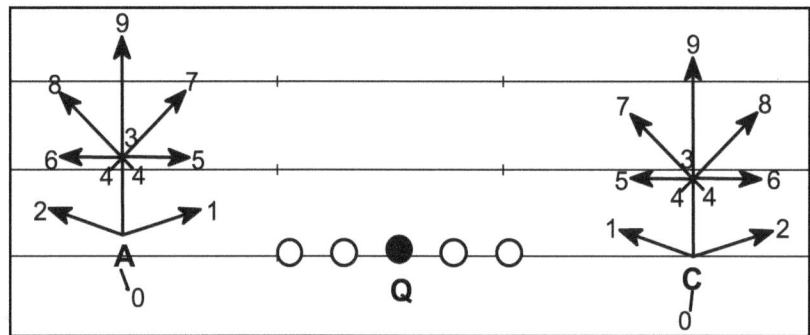

Long Tree

- Add 9 in front of the route
- Same as short tree with one change: the vertical release/stem is twice as long; 6-step vertical release – double the short tree
- routes 3 – 8 are re-named with a "9" in front
- 9 means "6-step vertical release" – 93, 94, 95, 96, 97, 98
- Routes 0, 1, 2, 9 remain single digits, 9 never precedes these single digit routes
- Long tree routes are pronounced by using "**ninety**" (i.e. ninety-seven, not nine-seven)

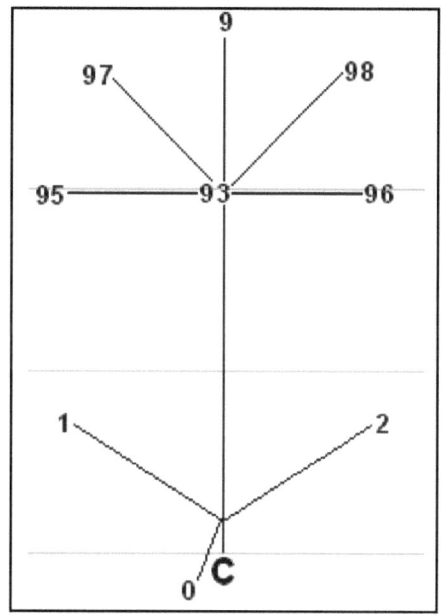

Combination/Unlimited Tree

- This tree forms limitless routes by combining short tree and long tree routes, using 2 or 3 digits
- The same rules apply as in short and long tree procedure.
- Combination routes are designated by either a 2-digit or 3-digit number.

2-Digit Combination Routes

Two digits from the short tree may be combined to form one route.

15/17 Exceptions

The digit "1" in a "15" or "17" combination route represents an exception to the 3-step vertical release rule. The digit "1" means "no vertical release." Instead, the 1st step is either at 30° (15) or 75° (75).

15 pattern – "15" (pronounced "fifteen")

This combines a "slant" and "in" to form a crossing route where the receiver sprints almost horizontally (30° angle to the LOS). The receiver's first step is a 30° step with the inside foot, followed by a sprint at a 30° angle.

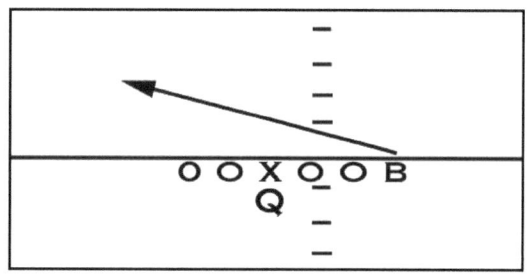

17 pattern – "17" (pronounced "seventeen")

Combines a "slant" and "post" to create a no-vertical release 75° sprint to the post. The receiver's first step is 75° with the inside foot, followed by a sprint at a 75° angle.

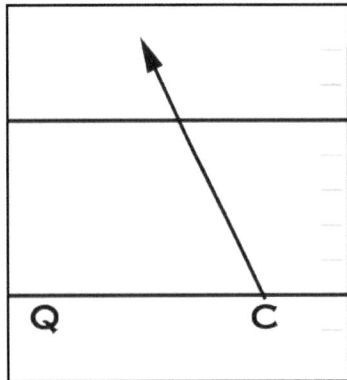

Example: *75* (pronounced "*seventy-five*"): **7** conveys "post"; **5** conveys "in"; Result is a "dig" pattern

There are **3 paths** in this combined route:

Vertical Lane – Stem.

Turning Lane – 3-step break and direction change.

Speedway – Final path to target area.

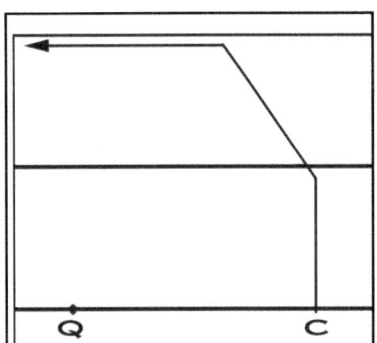

- **Lane 1: Vertical lane** — Refers to the stem, an up-field sprint. The length is determined by the presence or absence of "9." Without a "9," the vertical release is 3 steps (same as short tree). The rationale for exactly 3 or 6 steps is timing. They coincide with short and deep QB drops.

- **Lane 2: Turning Lane** — This is a 3-step path. Against man coverage, it is intended to turn (flip) the man-cover defenders hips (open the defender). Against zone, it is intended to allow the receiver to search for a seam.

- **Lane 3: Speedway** — Refers to the final path leading to the reception point. The distance of this path is dictated by the length of the QB's drop, degree of QB protection, and extent of QB's search through read progression.

3-Digit Combination Routes

Three digits from the short tree may be combined to form one route.

Example: 29-8 ("*twenty-nine eight*") 2 = slant out; 9 = 3-step vertical; 8 = corner.

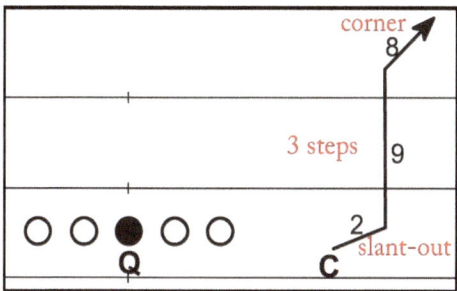

Behind-LOS Routes / Negative Routes — The area behind the LOS is the negative area, meaning it represents no gain.

The LOS and the area behind it are vital pass-reception areas that lead to positive gain. Our negative routes represent an extension of our running game. The following diagram is not a separate tree, it's incorporated in the combo tree. Negative routes are 2-digit patterns that attack the LOS and behind it. These routes center on 0, 1, 2 – hitch, slant in, slant out. The following are derivates that stem from combining these 3 routes:

- 10: Directly on LOS to QB – 1(slant to) + zero(hitch) = straight online to QB.
- 20: Directly on LOS away from QB – 2(slant away) + zero(hitch) = straight online to QB
- 01: 45-degrees slant back to QB – zero(hitch) + 1(slant to) = reverse slant to QB.
- 02: 45-degrees slant back away from QB – zero(hitch) + 2(slant away) = reverse slant away from QB.

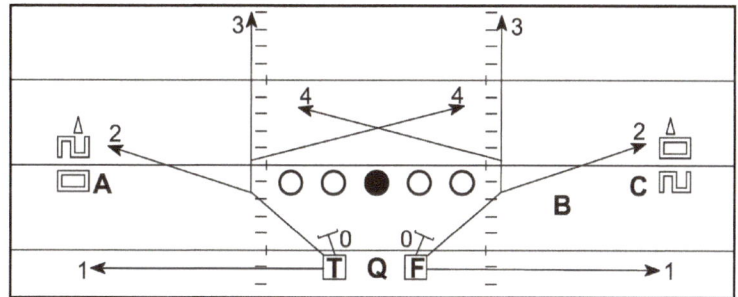

RB Route Tree

TB = Release to left; FB = Release to right.

0 = Block (no blitz – release to 1/Flare)

1 = Flare

2 = Flat

3 = Fly

4 = Cross

"5" in front of route means "release to opposite side" (e.g., "51").

Patterns may be combined (example):

    01 = Screen

    12 = Flare and Fly

    23 – flat and fly

    32 – fly and out

    30 – fly and freeze/sit in window

Limitless Tree

The pass route capacity is limitless. The limitless capacity makes a one-page diagram impossible. The following is a sample of its potential:

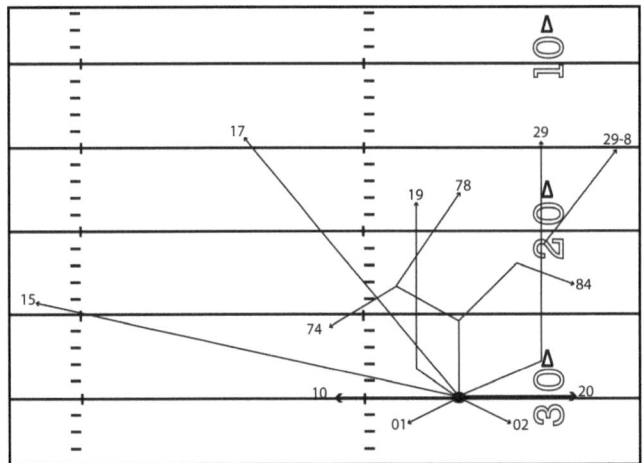

ELEMENT 9

Hole Numbers – Intended Points of Running Attack (IPOA)

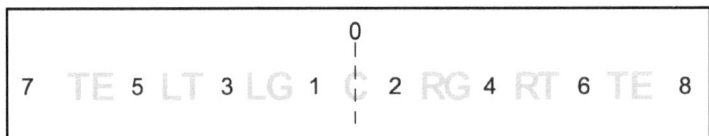

ELEMENT 10

Run Blocking Concepts/Rules

The chart below explains the run blocking concepts and run play-calling.

Family	Concept			General Blocking Scheme
1st	0 → 1 → 2			KO / Trap Drive & Steer
2nd	7 Stretching Play / Outside Zone	→	5 Inside Zone	Zone
3rd	Option ↓ Freeze (208, 388)	→	Zone Read (188, 178)	Zone
4th	3 → FSG Pull	4 → FST Pull	11 BSG & FSG Pulls	KO/Trap Drive & Steer

Summary

The following is a review of how to apply the SWAT dictionary and language to the Base Stretch Pass which I use as my teaching point-of-reference.

Building and Calling the Base Stretch Pass

Step 1: Call Temporary Formation – "*Quick Gun Bravo 5*".

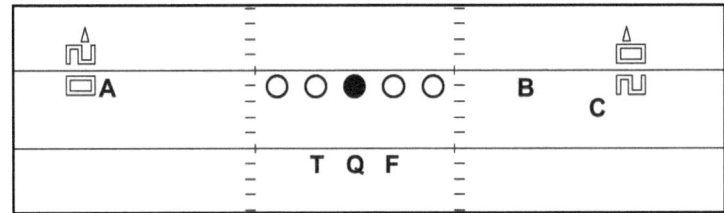

Step 2: Call Shift/Motion for Defense Recognition – "*Mike 2*".

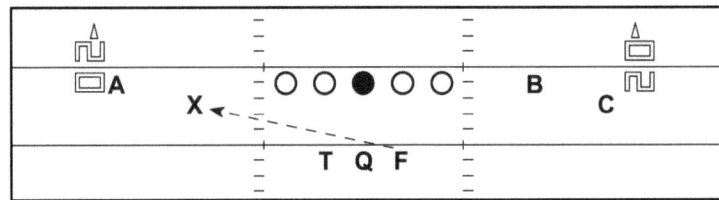

Step 3: Call Frontside Pass Routes – "*Bravo Charlie 8-95*".

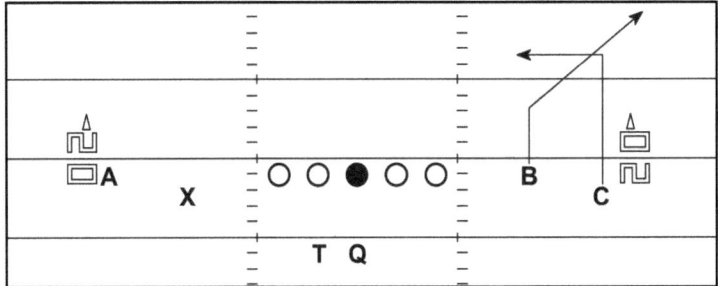

Step 4: Call Backside Pass Routes – "*17, 15, zero*" (Alpha, X-Ray, Tango) left to right to backfield.

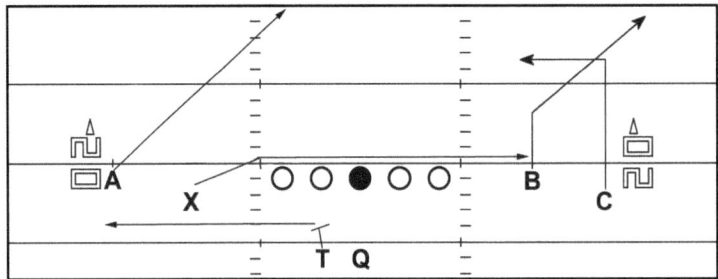

Chapter 3: Decision-Making Models

SCORES + 5-S

This chapter explains two decision-making models. SCORES is for coaches only, to introduce what will be taught later in the system. The 5-S model is taught to quarterbacks first. Reason: SCORES is the coverage-recognition model and the QB play-calling model. QBs are taught to read coverage and call their own plays after 5-S.

Play-calling is decision-making. It makes or breaks careers. In policing, the second worst label you can be pasted with is the dreaded "can't make a decision." The worst label is "chickenshit"... "coward". These two labels share the same DNA – fear. Fear that is never managed, never conquered... the type that causes freezing or fleeing instead of fighting, and ultimately incompetence.

The secret to conquering the decision-making fear and mystery is experience plus structure. Decision-making reps, falling on your ass, getting scraped, getting up, learning what went wrong, fixing it, and do it again until you don't blink. The worst thing a coordinator can do is blink. The sound of a blink is deafening. The most intellectually-challenged player can hear it. The blink label is the football version of the top two dreaded police labels.

Like all decision-making, making the right call needs information. Like crime-fighting, motive and opportunity is the formula for decision-making success. Have a reason for what you decide and base the reason from research that builds an opening.

Winging it is the uninformed decision-making trap that's easy to fall in to. The rush starts, when things aren't going well, and especially when things start falling apart. But, winging it is disastrous – it fixes nothing. Uniformed decisions are blind decisions – winging it instead of bringing it. And, decision-making needs a GPS – a model to guide the decision-making process.

The SWAT play-calling is governed by the SCORES decision-making model. It's a step-by-step formula to make the right call by identifying the problem and reaching a solution.

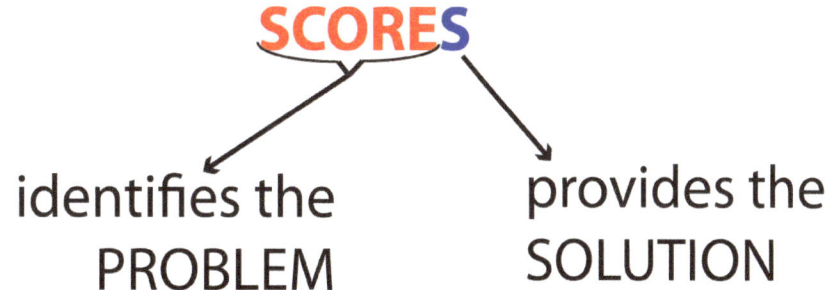

This diagram shows the general plan – what **SCORES** is intended to do. Solve a problem – what call to make is a specific situation. Justifying a decision instead of winging it.

The model can't be learned all at once. It's learned in stages.

∞

What was and what is connects with what will be.

Managing a football game is exactly like leading a major crime investigation. No difference. Both are problem-solving exercises intended to solve mysteries. High-speed thinking, rapid decision-making, and all the while dealing with the human element. Facing uncertainty, finding out what needs to be known, gather information, process it, keep the relevant, discard the irrelevant. I borrowed an investigative philosophy from my detective career – an investigation connects evidence, belief and the call.

To make any call, you need to connect what you know and what it means to what you'll do. Connect *what was* with *what is* with *what will be*.

Here's how we do it.

The SCORES Decision-Making Model

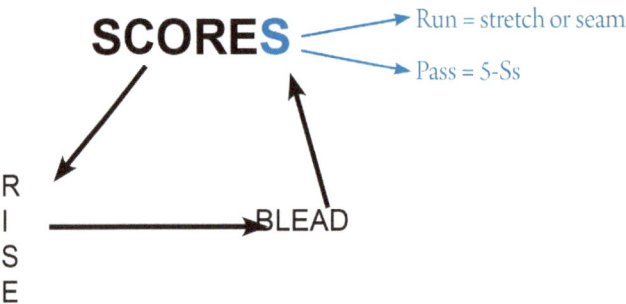

SCORE = SCan + Observe + REcognize

The S represents the decision – pass or run. S stands for **5-S model** of pass play building and stretch or seam model for run play building.

SCORES has 2 elements. SCORE represents the thinking – the decision-making process. S is the decision – run or pass – and how to design it.

SCORES governs play-calling by the OC and/or QB. The model shows a clockwise chain of thinking that starts with scanning plus observing, leading to a call of pass or run, and how to design the call. How to make the call, how to build it.

SCORES operates clockwise but it's taught/learned in reverse – counter-clockwise. The starting point is the 5-Ss at the far right of the model. 5-Ss governs how to design unlimited SWAT passes. It's the center of SWAT teaching and learning. Then, we work backwards. Before the 5-Ss is taught, the language is introduced – definitions of **scores, rise, blead, stretch or seam, 5 Ss.**

∞

SCORE = SCan + Observe + REcognize

- Scan and observe gathers the defensive information. Recognize translates it.
- The blue **S** at the end means solution… the call – pass or run.
- **Stretch** or **Seam** is the running play model – 2 classifications of running plays and a model that governs how to design them.

- **5 Ss is the pass play model** – a 5-step model that governs how to design unlimited pass plays without a playbook and without a huddle, within 8 seconds.
- SCORE defines the problem – what the defense intends to do.
- S solves it by selecting the right call.

∞

RISE is the decision-making model that governs 'how to' scan + observe.
- R — Realign
- I — Imagery
- S — Situation
- E — Evaluation

BLEAD is the decision-making models that guides 'how to' Recognize the Image – how to read the defensive alignment.
- B — Box
- L — Level 4 defenders
- E — Eyes
- A — Alignment
- D — Depth

∞

Stretch/Seam corresponds to the Running Play Chart. How to apply the running play chart is taught after the **5-S** passing model is installed (*explained in the next SWAT book*).

∞

The key to SWAT unlimited passing is the 5-S decision-making model. 5-S is the decision-making model that governs 'how to' design a pass play:

5-S Model

- **S**eparate at least 4 receivers from defenders. ⎫ *Spacing*
- **S**eparate at least 4 receivers from receivers. ⎭

- **S**ame sight line. Position as many receivers as possible in one field of vision to facilitate the search for open receiver. ⎫
- **S**teer the safeties. (i) Open the middle of the field, or (ii) open the corner. Move the safety or keep him there. Bind or occupy safeties – force a decision and give them no choice. Steer with eyes or occupy with a receiver. ⎬ *Search*
  ⎭

- **S**afety valve. Minimum one hot receiver per pass play. ⎫ *QB Security*

Spacing, **S**earch, **S**ecurity... the 3 outcomes of the 5-S model. Any call, any situation... same model.

Spacing

Two types of separation are needed:

(i) receivers from themselves — a minimum 3-yard open radius around every receiver at the time of the throw – a halo. Never bunch 2 receivers downfield at the time of release.

(ii) receivers from defenders — open receivers is an abstract concept. We define it concretely as an isolated receiver, where the ball's closing time is faster than the defender's closing time. A receiver is isolated/open when the defender's closing distance is farther than the ball's closing distance.

Search

Xs and Os are useless unless the QB can discover open receivers. The QB's mindset and balls are the biggest factors. To help the QB develop both, the play design has to be conducive with search development. Young QBs can't be expected to search for receivers while being pursued by a pack of nasty rushers. Receiver selection and avoiding getting maimed are two separate and conflicting thought processes. The secret is simplifying each one separately… one at a time. ==Pass Rush Management== *is the secret to QB development*. It starts with arranging receivers in a way that's compatible with RDM (rapid decision-making) – the complexity of vision, eye movement, and thinking under pressure. ==Alignment== is the key. Alignment of receivers – downfield positioning has to make sense… purposeful positioning to facilitate the search. Build a simple field of vision – same sight line… put the pieces on a manageable board.

The search and same sight line are connected to steering the deep safeties. Whether there are one or two safeties, our philosophy and theory is the same:

(a) Influencing the positioning and movement of the safeties is key to explosive deep passing.

(b) The two ways to do it are by binding or occupying. Move or freeze the safeties with the QB eyes or receivers – force the safety to make a call, decide on one of two receivers, or give the safety no choice but to stay and cover in one place.

Opening the deep middle is top priority – it guarantees a TD or big play. But closing the middle intentionally opens the corner.

Security

Nothing is more important to passing. A secure, protected QB makes a coach look like the proverbial genius. Security is deeply connected to search. Search time and search proficiency dramatically increase when the QB is protected. But we don't use conventional definitions for protection and security. For example, we never use maximum protection. Not once in my career have we kept a tight end in to block. We believe in 46 and 55 security because the QB must be part of the security team. He has to avoid sacks and not rely exclusively on blocking. Here are the 4 SWAT Security Principles:

- The re-definition of "hot receiver": any route that has reception points at every step of the route.
- The re-definition of "discretionary QB drop": our primary focus is the 5-step drop. Nothing is rigid or fixed in the SWAT system. The QB has discretion to change it to 3 or 7 depending on the threat level.

- The re-definition of "QB as a ballcarrier": he is expected to run, not scramble. He is expected to never throw the ball away. He is expected to think deep – on the field and inside his mind. Changing the vocabulary changes the mindset. Changing the mindset changes the outcome.

- Instead of keeping people in to block pressure, we throw pressure on the defense. Fight pressure with more pressure… and see who cracks first.

Chapter 4: Stretch Pass

The Stretch Pass is the starting point of the SWAT Offense – the center of the system… the instruction point-of-reference used to teach and apply the SWAT language and decision-making models.

The Stretch Pass is not one play. The stretch pass is a tactic – a group of plays that uses 4-5 receivers to:

- stretch the defense vertically and horizontally creating a void in the middle,
- connecting 2 partial concepts – frontside (FS) and backside(BS) – into a full concept,
- forming overload FS – BS ratios, ie: 41 ratio – 4 receivers in FS, one BS, and
- building a consistent image.

The Stretch Pass PLOWs – Positions, Lengthens, Opens, and Widens. The Stretch Pass pushes the defense past its limits vertically and horizontally, opening the main border (LOS), building secondary open borders (middle), while positioning receivers in searchable groups – building multi-level 90-degree frontsides.

The Stretch Pass series build a consistent image, the key to finding open receivers. Similar images teach how to see the whole board instead of one piece at a time. The objectives of the Stretch Pass are go deep or go wide…throw more pressure than you receive.

The Base Image

The BASE Stretch Pass is the connection of the first 2 partial concepts. It forms the following image:

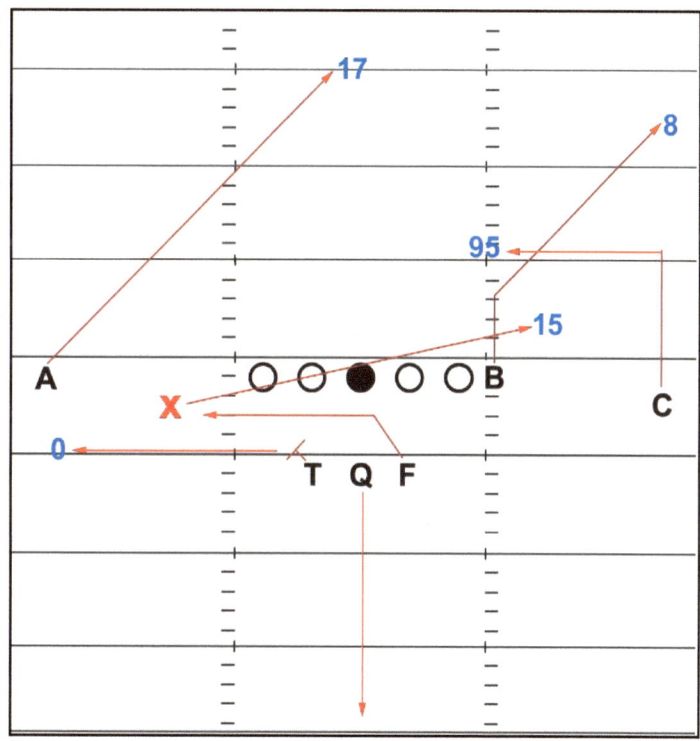

STRETCH PASS – Theory

The Stretch Pass spreads deep and wide low, opening the middle with a 41 FS-BS ratio (4 receivers grouped on the frontside, one on the backside), with a 3-level spacing (short, deep, middle) using a 46 or 55 protection (4 receivers and 6 blockers or 5 receivers and 5 blockers).

The Stretch Pass builds a 3-way, 3-direction stretch (vertical and 2 horizontal levels – short and middle) with a minimum of 80% of receivers in a half-field same sight line, attacking four zone-busting and 4 man-busting places.

The four seams attacked are:

(i)   low flat, a horizontal seam near the LOS;

(ii) middle horizontal seam separating deep and short zones;

(iii) middle deep seam; and

(iv) numbers seam.

The four man-busting places attacked are: post, corner, low flat, middle lane.

In SWAT language, the Base Stretch Pass is called **Bravo Charlie 8-95**. Translation:

- this is a pass play;
- Bravo runs 8 pattern, Charlie runs 95 pattern;
- 8-95 is a partial concept – Smash Bind (corner-in);
- this partial concept is the frontside of the play; and
- the QB will complete the play at the LOS, calling the backside routes by simply filling in the blanks from left to right – telling each receiver his assignment.

Pass plays are called by starting the play with a receiver code name – e.g., Bravo, Charlie. Running plays are called with a 3-digit number, e.g., 367. All 5 receivers have a code name: **Alpha, Bravo, Charlie, Foxtrot, Tango**. Foxtrot changes to X-Ray if he motions from the FB spot (the FX effect) to outside the box. The offensive coordinator (OC) and quarterback (QB) collaborate at the LOS to build a play using the same decision-making model, called the 5-S model. Plays are not memorized from a playbook. They are built at the LOS, communicated, and translated. Memorization is replaced by translation. After the QB masters the decision-making model, he makes the entire call himself. Until then the OC and QB are play-calling partners.

Stretch Pass – Summary

1 — **Two directions** – toward and away from the sideline.

2 — **Depth levels** (deep, middle, short).

3 — **46 or 55 security/protection means:** (a) 4 receiver release + 6 blockers protect, (b) 5 receivers release + 5 blockers. Stretch the defense, tight security.

4 — **41 FS/BS ratio means:** 4 receivers connect into the 90-degree right frontside with

only one receiver on the backside. Those 4 receivers are positioned at **3 depth levels**, in **2 directions** (to the right sideline + away from the right sideline). All 5 receivers are spaced properly – no two receivers are clustered together within a 5-yard radius. Three frontside receivers are aligned on the same sight line. The fourth is in the periphery. Maximum security protects the QB – 46 protection (33 BOB) plus 2 hot receivers, plus a 5-step drop that can change to 7 or 9 or more into a structured QB rollout. And the depth of the shotgun snap can change to beyond 5 yards. It is impossible for all four frontside receivers to be "covered" – regardless of coverage, the combined effect of those 4 routes beats any man or zone. Our research shows that a minimum of 2 receivers will always be open in every pass play. ==The key is having the QB search for and find them.== When that happens, any pass play will work.

B.O.M.B. – QB SWAT Read: Best Open Man Board
The Board Theory.

SWAT QB Read

See the whole board,

Know the situation,

Make the call,

Remember it.

I don't believe a novice, amateur QB can look at 4 or 5 receivers in sequence, one at a time, to find an open receiver. The reason is my own personal research – analyzing our practices, our game film, and most importantly, interviews with our QBs – supported by scientific research.[4] I documented a number of case studies, from my personal experience, and researched three empirical studies footnoted below. The conclusion I reached was that young QBs **Build IQ** — they see an Image and they develop Instinct. Combining Image and Instinct builds QB expertise in finding open receivers.

This is how it works: QBs view an area, scan it, recognize who is open, and decide on what move to make – the call... which receiver to select (the best open man on the board that fits the situation), they press SAVE and file it in their mental database, building neural pathways that will make finding open receivers an automatic, second-nature response.

In other words, they see pictures... moving pictures that keep getting bigger with practice. They see the big picture, not each individual in the picture. They start with a wide focus and narrow that focus down, not vice-versa. QBs don't start with a narrow focus and then expand it. With experience, they see wider images and recognize the uncovered man. This means they see the whole board, not individual pieces. Once the board is scanned they identify an open man within the framework of the big picture – image analysis. And then they burn it into long-term memory until the B.O.M.B. becomes instinctive – automatic, second-nature.

I stopped teaching a read progression. I stopped numbering downfield receivers. No more viewing order. No primary receivers. No secondary receivers. No high, low, check down. Instead of looking at a progression of receivers in order of priority, I started teaching QBs to select receivers on every deep pass by scanning the **B.O.M.B. – Best Open Man Board.**

See the whole board,

Know the situation,

Make the call,

Remember it.

---

4 The "see the board, know the situation, make a call, remember it" theory was initially based on our documented case studies and supported by three prominent sources that have been cited in scientific journals: (i) de Groot, A.D. (1978). Thought and Choice in Chess (Rev. Translation, 1946; 2nd ed). The Hague, the Netherlands: Mouton. (ii) the "Template Theory" published by: Gobet, F and Simon, H.A. (1996a). Templates in Chess Memory: A Mechanism for Recalling Several Boards. Cognitive Psychology, 31, 1-40. (iii) Leonard, Dorothy, Swap, Walter C. (2005) Deep Smarts. Harvard Business Press. I strongly recommend that all coaches read Deep Smarts especially those who strive to become coordinators.

I grouped as many receivers as possible into one sight line, forming an easily viewable board. Every practive rep is always connected to a situation – no exception. Every drill has a situation, whether it's 1-on-1, 3-on-3, 7-on-7, 11-on-11. The situation became part of the board, not separate from it. Then, make the call... select a receiver by scanning the picture and making a decision by recognizing open receivers and selecting the best one that fits the situation – identifying them within the framework of the image. The secret to making the right call is ==equalizing the value of every pass route.== All pass routes are created equally. Short or long, all pass routes are intended to do the same thing – go deep. The key is run and block after the catch. YAC doesn't just tilt the playing field, it makes it lopsided. We don't believe in the myth of the first down pass, the short pass... the stereotype pass. The distance of the throw is different but not the outcome. Short, medium or long, every pass completion has the same value – the potential to go deep. No completion is wrong. Every completion is the right call. If the catch doesn't result in a first down or touchdown, the blocking and running *after the catch* failed. This mindset works wonders – it spikes completion percentage, passing yards, and points. YAC dramatically changes the game in favor of the offense. The reason why YAC is explosive and easier to gain than running plays is the **pursuit angle challenge**, referring to the difficulty that defenders experience in choosing the correct pursuit angle following a catch. Unlike run plays, pass plays don't allow repeatable or predictable pursuit angles that can be practiced with certainty during preparation. Each reception forms a unique situation — a unique starting point with different places where the ball-carrier and defenders align to race to the goal line. In other words, it's impossible to practice every conceivable passing situation to teach pursuit angles against every possible catch. Add a fatigued defense and catching the ball at full sprint, the YAC potential grows exponentially. The possibilities are limitless. No completion is wrong. The pressure is off the QB.

4 Levels: Receiver Depths

A level is defined as a distance in relation to the LOS. The Base Stretch Pass 4 depth levels are:

Level 1 – behind the LOS

Level 2 – short

Level 3 – intermediate

Level 4 – deep

The final product has 4 receivers in the frontside, at 3 different levels, in one sight line. One receiver in the backside builds the 4-level structure.

Same Sight Line

Two-part definition:

(i) *Exact* **same sight line** is the exact straight alignment of receivers at 3 levels. Exact alignment occurs momentarily – only for a second, where all three receivers cross an imaginary QB's vision line that forms a 45-degree angle to the LOS. A number of factors affect the exact alignment of 3 receivers including receiver speed and coverage which dictates pattern detours – adjusted routes.

(ii) *General* **same sight line** is the inexact alignment of 3-levels of receivers. This inexact alignment occurs within the framework of the 90-degree FS that can be easily scanned.

Two-Direction Sight Line

The 3 receivers on the exact same sight line move in two directions – *to* sideline, *away* from sideline. The corner and flat are to the sideline. The middle-in is away from the sideline.

Pass Protection: Big on Big – 3x3

No-huddle, limited practice hours, one-man staff means simple blocking. The Base Stretch Pass starts with 46 security (4 receivers + 6 blockers) divided into 3x3 big-on-big pass protection, that may change to 55 security (5 receivers + 5 blockers) while the play is in progress.

Rules:

(i) OL blocks covered DL = level 1 defenders, numbered starting at 1 outside to the center.

LT blocks #1

LG blocks #2

CTR blocks #3 to right or on midline

RT blocks #1

RG blocks #2

TB block #3 (offline blitzer)

(ii) Center blocks away from the single-back. He receives his instruction by the motion/shift codeword during the cadence: MIKE means FB motions – TB on left blocks left, center blocks right. DELTA means TB motions – FB on right blocks right, center blocks left.

(iii) In the Base Stretch, the TB has a ZERO pass route assignment, meaning discretionary release. Discretionary release means: TB looks in, looks out, releases to flare – and never double-teams. If rusher #6 goes, TB stays. If only 5 or less rush, TB goes.

The frontside forms the **whole board** with 4 receivers. 3 receivers are scanned in one exact sight line (corner, middle-in, low flat) and the fourth entering the post from the backside, forming a general same sight line.

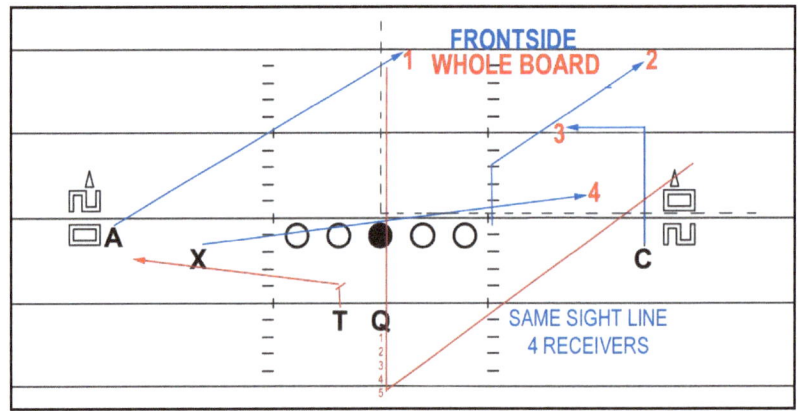

The blue shade represents the primary scan. The red shade shows the secondary scan. No primary receiver. All are potential primary receivers. Open receivers are discernible while scanning the whole board as opposed to reading high, then low.

See the whole board:

- Scan the FS IMAGE. View the same sight line.

Know the situation:

- Score, down, distance, personnel, habits (theirs and ours).

Make the call:

(a) Find and throw to best open man in FS, or

(b) look to BS, or

(c) run.

I never teach *"throw the ball away."* I've never said this statement to any QB in my life and never will because:

(i) it teaches a bad habit – throwing to open air is not a learning outcome in our system;

(ii) it gives license to make an unnatural throw that will get intercepted;

(iii) it removes focus from running; and

(iv) without it, only positive-gain alternatives are left to consider – complete the pass or run. Two perfomance demands. No option for failure.

Scanning FS to BS

The QBs eyes are defensive reads, keys to interceptions. There are 3 ways to scan FS to BS:

i. FS – BS only. Look only at the FS. If no receivers are open, look to BS.

ii. MOF to FS-BS. MOF means middle of the field. Look directly at the deep midline at the Free Safety (FS) position. Then, scan frontside to backside. The dual-purpose of this search is: (a) to determine MOFO/MOFC – is the middle of the field open or closed? (b) freeze the free safety – intentionally create MOFC. Keeping the middle of the field closed opens the corner.

iii. BS 1/3 to FS-BS. First look at backside 1/3, then scan FS/BS. The purpose is to steer the free safety and open the middle of the field – creating MOFO.

The same applies to 2 free safeties. Nothing changes.

Chapter 5: Limitless Formations

During my 40-season coaching career, I have seen first-hand how the majority of our opponents limit themselves to a handful of standard formations as if there was a template that governed how formations had to be designed. Cookie-cutter formations with 11 statues lined up motionless in exactly the same formations passed on from generation to generation. The power of conformity cannot be understated. Conformity is a force of nature – and nurture. It keeps people motionless, restricting forward progress because of fear of perceived, wrongly-defined risk and uncertainty.

Football evolves slowly because too many football coaches are followers, not innovators. Original thinking is missing from football because, like many professions, coaches are immobilized by the fear of being different. The result is the copycat syndrome which leads to lack of imagination which leads to confusing strategy for rules.

Football is governed by a mythology that has made up formulas for winning based on anecdotal evidence. Then it spread unchallenged as the truth. Two examples of bullshit are: (i) running wins championships, and (ii) finesse passing teams. The only reason why running won a lot of championships is because that's what most teams did – the path of least resistance. Including me back in the 1980s. But the biggest bullshit of all is the myth of the finesse passing team. 100% bullshit. Passing is not finesse, it's a power game. A pound and ground game. Pass blocking and downfield blocking in open space after a catch are more of a power game than run blocking. And I have the evidence to prove it. Contrary to popular myth, passing in a warp-speed no-huddle is the true way to steamroll and flatten any opponent, including Goliaths. Hit hard, hit fast. That's what our no-huddle passing does. It hits harder and faster than any ground game can produce for us.

I've been blessed to have worked outside of football, in real life where originality is needed to survive. Investigate a solution for your unique challenges. Some solutions are universal. Some aren't. Finding the truth that works for you takes the guts to experiment within your own reality, even at the expense of eyebrow raising. Overcoming the fear of critics is the single-most important X Factor that solves the mystery of what works in your situation.

There isn't one formation that we can't build at the LOS. The SWAT language lets us call any formation possible without having to memorize even one page of formations. We don't name formations. We don't have pages of diagrammed formations to memorize. We build them at the LOS by literally telling players where to align and where to move. ==Memorization is replaced by translation.==

We take advantage of two basic offensive rules:

1) the two ends can align online anywhere from the tackles to the sideline; and

2) offline players (backfield players one yard behind the LOS) can line up anywhere from sideline-to-sideline and at any depth behind the LOS.

It makes no sense to limit ourselves by aligning at expected places in expected formations. The width of an American field is 53.3 yards wide. A Canadian field is not on par – it's an enormous 65 yards wide. There's enormous land mass behind the LOS. For decades, football teams chose to not take advantage of these two simple rules and the size of available real estate. We do. And it's not complicated nor does it complicate our offense. Limitless formations do not contradict our basic philosophy — don't ignore simplicity. It fits right in.

Limitless formations have a purpose. It's not about '*My playbook is bigger than yours.*' There are two major benefits of limitless formations – show it and blow it:

i) **Intelligence-Gathering**. Defenses telegraph their intention when we use shifts/motion to build formations in stages in full view of the defense at the LOS.

ii) **Pressure**. Shifting/motioning 80 times a game, each one in 8 seconds, builds mental and physical pressure on a defense, tiring out mind and body. Our 8-second rule creates a thinking race. A high speed test on every play. We wear you out by forcing you to solve a mystery with a time-limit. Having to match up to formation changes at warp speed causes mistakes. Mental fatigue. Then there is the physical fatigue through long distance running. Shifting and motion is physically tiring. It adds significant distances that defenders have to run in a game. We can add about to 800 extra yards of running per game. Defenses don't have the energy to match it. It's outside their comfort zone. They don't prepare for it. Their practice reps are passive in comparison to ours.

We can build any conceivable formation – 3-backs, 2-backs, 1-back, no-backs. We use role reversal by switching our outside receivers and inside receivers. First we spread our 'wide' receivers wider than normal and then shrink them, aligning them at tight end and hiding them inside the box while spreading our Big Ends. Eventually, labels disappear. We are never bound by conventional names of offensive positions. In our system, "*wide receiver*" is a slang term. So is "*tight end*". Our receivers have to learn to align at every conceivable spot online, offline, spread, tight, in the box, or in the backfield regardless of the player's size and shape.

It's impossible to study us on film. You'll never identify our tendencies. You'll never connect a formation to a specific play with 100% certainty. The number of formations we use in a season makes it impossible to prepare for every formation because no defense has enough time during a week to invest scout team reps for every formation that we are capable and willing to use. And we can't be profiled because we use a wide range of formations to run the same plays. We never ignore simplicity – it only looks like we do.

We can build any formation by simply communicating the SWAT language in two stages: (i) call a temporary or starting formation; and (ii) build a final formation with shift/motion. The entire process takes 2-4 seconds. The key is to make the call immediately after the previous plays ends. Not one second of delay. Quick thinking is critical. The entire system depends on rapid decision-making, making the call faster and better than the defense.

I stopped teaching limitless formations as a separate topic almost 20 years ago. It makes no sense to teach formations in isolation, separate from any other topic. I follow a teaching rule that I used in college law enforcement teaching – contextual teaching, a teaching strategy that incorporates scenario-based teaching. It's an instructional strategy where one scenario serves as the point-of-reference to which multiple learning outcomes connect. One example is using derivative Base Stretch Pass plays to teach limitless formation and the 5-S decision making model that governs the building of pass plays at the LOS.

Derivative Base Stretch Pass plays are plays that form the same or similar downfield images. Each one follows the 5-S model:

- Separate receivers from receivers. Avoid 2 receivers in close proximity.
- Separate receivers from defenders. Use partial concepts that have both man-buster and zone-buster capacity.
- Same sight line. Build a compact, viewable, easy-to-search board. Position as many receivers as possible in one observation area.
- Steer the safeties. Control safeties' decisions. Occupy safeties with a receiver or influence them with QB's eyes during the QB drop.
- Safety valve. Incorporate at least one hot receiver.

Limitless formations can't be taught all at once. It has to be taught in stages. Phase 1 is the first learning unit. Phase 1 includes 7 core formations combined with countless Base Stretch Pass plays. The following is what I teach:

Phase 1 – Limitless Formations

The 7 core formations in SWAT language and corresponding diagram are as follows:

1. I Bravo 4
2. Quick Gun Bravo 5
3. I Bravo 5
4. Quick Gun AC
5. I AC
6. Quick gun AC34
7. I AC 34

1 — I BRAVO 4

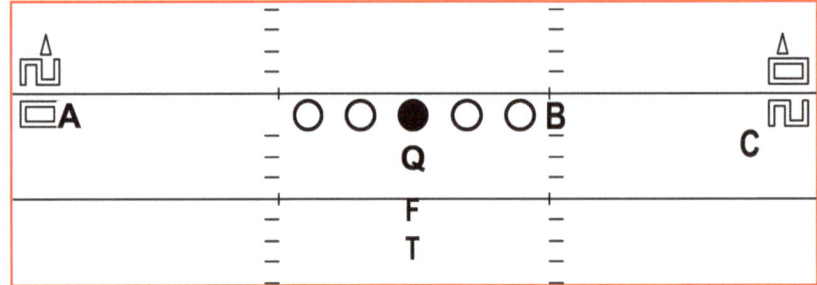

Translation
- Same as Quick Gun Bravo 4 except the QB aligns under center with a 2-back I.
- I = 2-back backfield formation.
- QB under center.
- FB and TB on the midline, 3 yards and 6 yards respectively.
- Bravo 4 = Alpha and Bravo are the online receivers. Charlie is offline.
- Bravo (TE) aligns at the 4 spot.
- Alpha online at the 1 spot.
- Charlie at 6 spot.

2 — Quick Gun Bravo 5

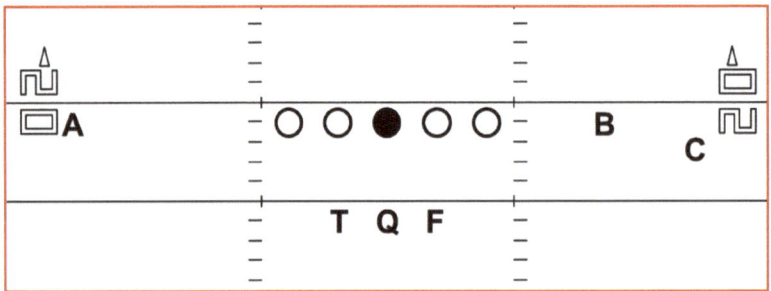

68

Translation:

- Same as Quick Gun Bravo 4 except TE is flexed right in a 2-pt stance
- Quick Gun = 2-back shotgun, 4-yard depth.
- TB and FB – both noses in B gap (guard/tackle gap).
- Bravo 5 = Alpha and Bravo are online. Charlie is offline.
- Alpha at 1 online.
- Bravo at 5 – 2-point stance, online slot (flex).
- Charlie at 6 offline.

3 — I Bravo 5

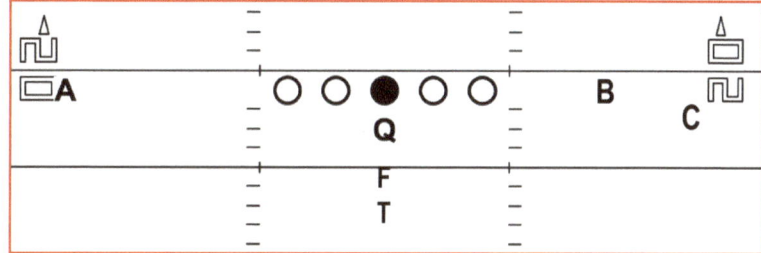

Translation:

- Same as Quick Gun Bravo 5 except 2-back I.

4 — Quick Gun AC

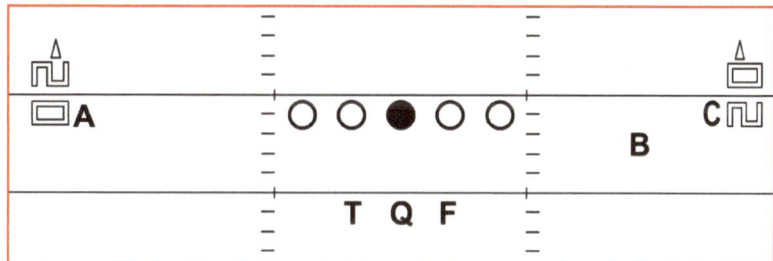

Translation:

- Same concept as Quick Gun Bravo 5 except Bravo and Charlie exchange online/offline positions.
- Quick Gun = same 2-back shotgun.
- AC = Alpha and Charlie are the online receivers at 1 and 6 respectively.
- Bravo is offline at 5 – right slot.

5 — I AC

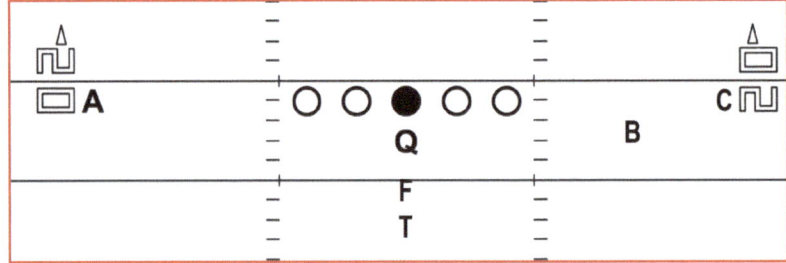

Translation:

- Same as Quick Gun AC expect the backfield.

6 — Quick Gun AC34

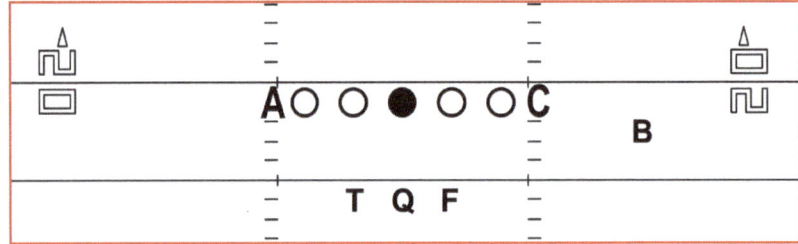

Translation:

- 2-back shotgun.
- - Alpha Charlie online, at 3 and 4 respectively – standup, 2 pt WRs at the TE spots.
- - Bravo offline at 5 (right slot).

7 — I AC 34

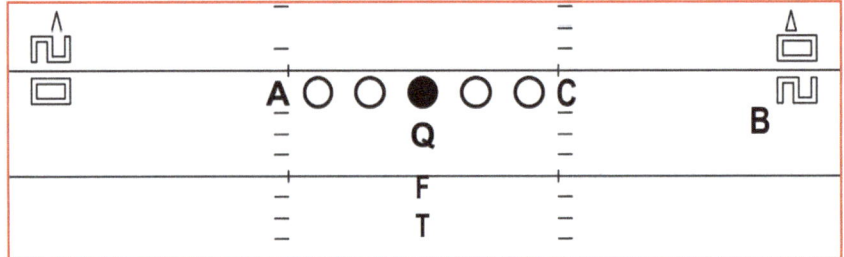

Translation:

- Same as Quick Gun AC 34 except backfield in I.
- Alpha and Charlie align at the conventional TE spots (3 and 4), standing up in 2-pt stances.

Key Points:

- All 7 phase 1 core formations are 21 1x2 formations:
    - 21 = 2 backs and one TE (Bravo).
    - 1x2 = one receiver on the left, 2 on the right.
- These 7 formations change to 11 (single-back + single-TE) and 01 (empty).
    - FB (Foxtrot) moves to the 4th receiver, becoming X if he aligns outside the box. TB (tailback) moves to 5th, retaining the code name Tango.
    - Mike plus a number means FB move to the new corresponding spot.
    - Delta plus a number means TB move to new corresponding spot.
- 1x2 changes by moving the offline receiver, using Lima or Oscar plus a number. Translation:
    - Lima instructs the offline right receiver to move Left to the corresponding number.
    - Oscar instructs the offline left receiver to move Right to the corresponding number.
- A conventional double-TE is not part of phase 1 – it is installed later. The AC formation resembles a double TE using the WR's instead, standing up in a 2-pt stance. This formation has produced explosive results.

How to Apply the Stretch Pass to Phase 1 Limitless Formations

Example #1 — Starting formation: Quick Gun Bravo 4 (base formation)

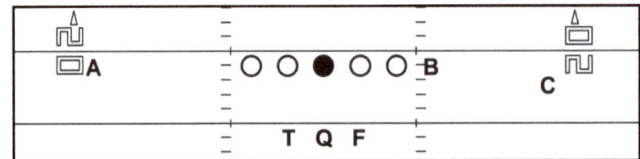

1st move: Mike 2   2nd move: Lima 3   3rd move: Oscar 5

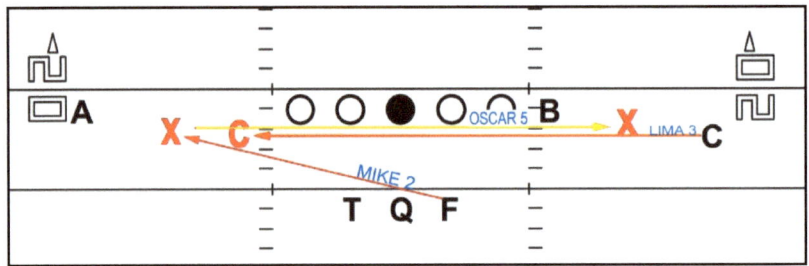

Make the Call: Bravo X-Ray 8-95: 17, 15, zero (same play)

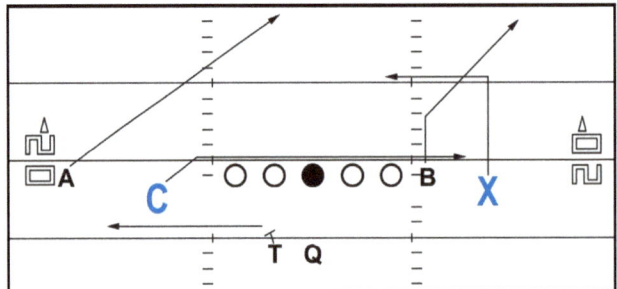

Key Points:

- First move changed the formation to an 11, 2x2.
- The 2nd move changed the formation to a tighter 11 2x2.
- X is in the right slot instead of right wide.
- C is at the left Inside Receiver spot, instead of slot left.
- The same play is called. The only difference will be the mesh point that aligns the 3 frontside receivers. Using a 5-step drop, the flat defender will be wider and the inside route will be inside the box.
- However, changing the QB drop to 3 steps aligns the frontside receivers.

Example #2 — Starting formation: I Bravo 4

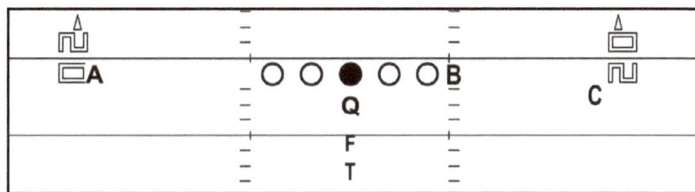

1st move: Mike 5   **2nd move: Lima 12**

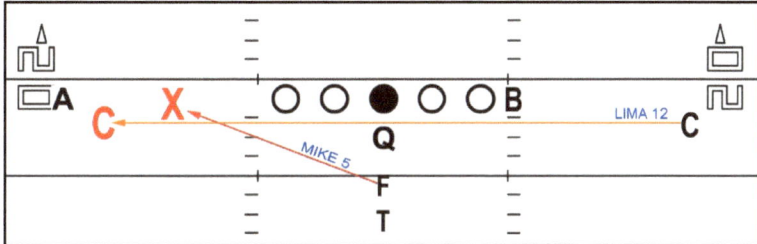

Make the Call: Bravo X-Ray 8-95: 17, 15, zero

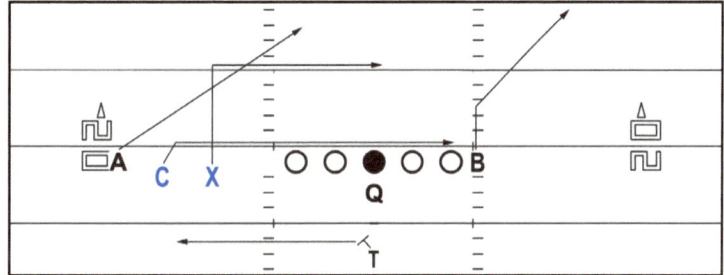

Key Points

- Same play with one major difference – the 2 left WRs are bunched.

Example #3 — Starting formation: Quick Gun Bravo 5

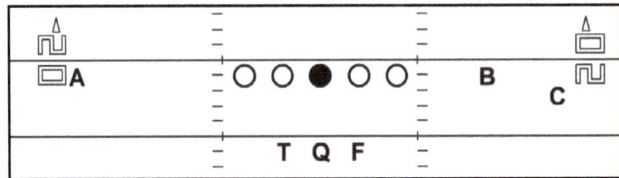

1st move: Mike 4

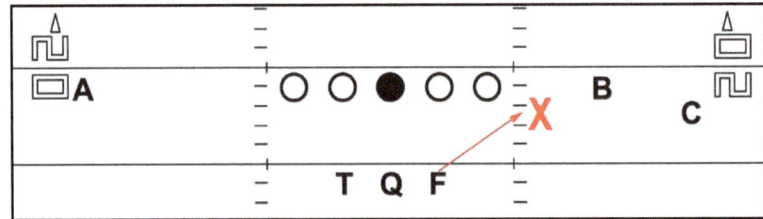

Make the Call: Bravo Charlie 8-95: 17, 26, zero

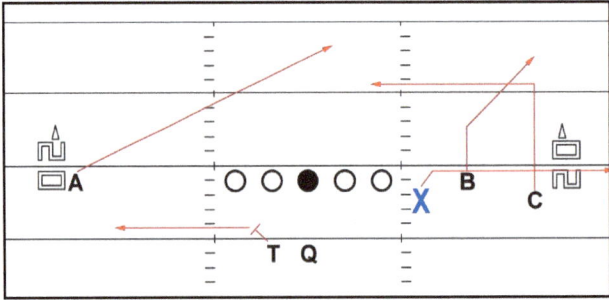

Key Points:

- Some of the benefits of flexing the TE include:
    » forces the defense to show its coverage ie: strong safety alignment;
    » changes the width of the corner pattern;
    » changes the track of the stretch running play to the right; and
    » easier to find vertical seams.
- To create the same image, a 1x3 is used and the flat is attacked with a 26 pattern, a frontside speed-out that has the same effect as a backside 15 pattern.
- The entire frontside is moved wider – farther from the QB and the box.

Example #4 — Starting formation: Quick Gun AC

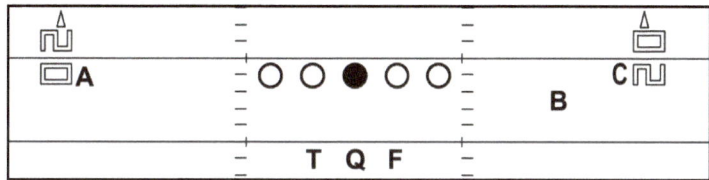

1st move: Lima 2   **2nd move: Mike 5**

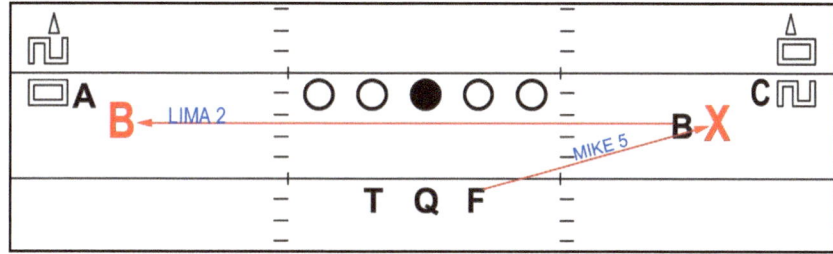

Make the Call: X-Ray Charlie 8-95: 17, 15, zero

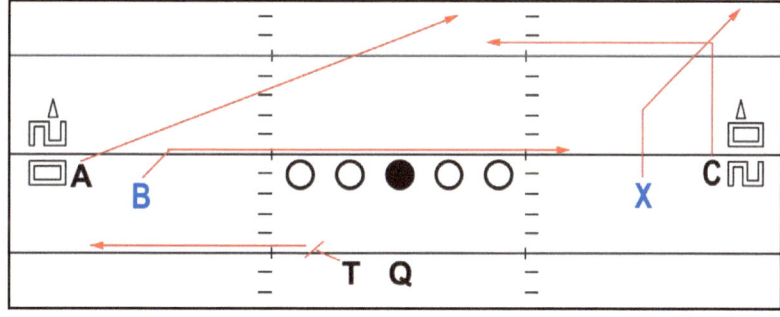

Key Points

- Same play except the in-pattern will be one yard deeper (Charlie is online) and the corner pattern will be shorter (X is offline).

Example #5 — Starting formation: Quick Gun AC34

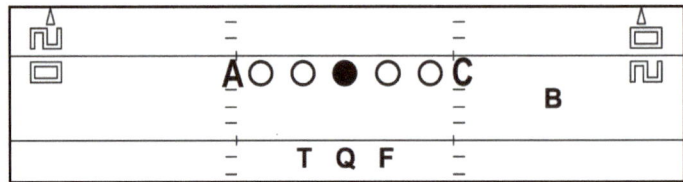

1st move: Mike 1

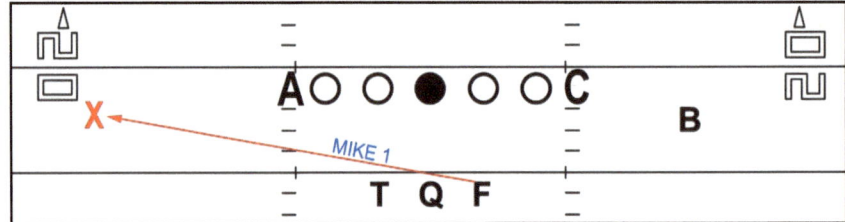

Make the Call: Charlie Bravo 8-95: 17, 15, zero (same play)

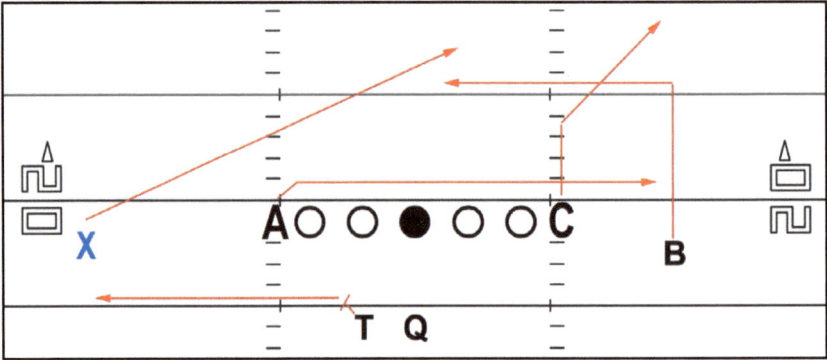

Key Points:

- Same play except the flat pattern (15) will be wider.
- The left WR (Alpha) is the #2 receiver aligned inside as a standup TE.
- Charlie and Bravo have exchanged assignments.

Example #6 same image, change 2 routes

Starting formation: Quick Gun AC34

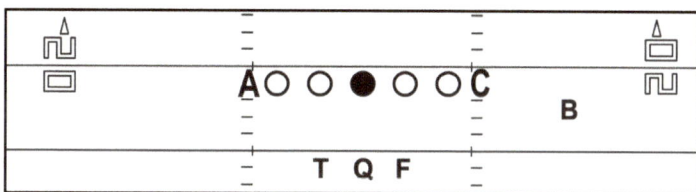

1st move: Mike 4   **2nd move: Lima 3**

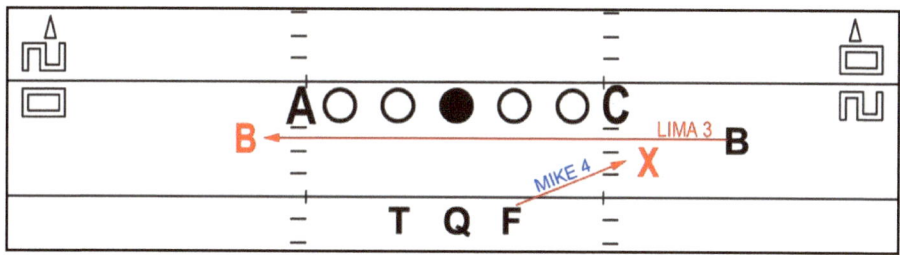

Make the call: Charlie X-Ray 8-29/5: 15, 9, zero

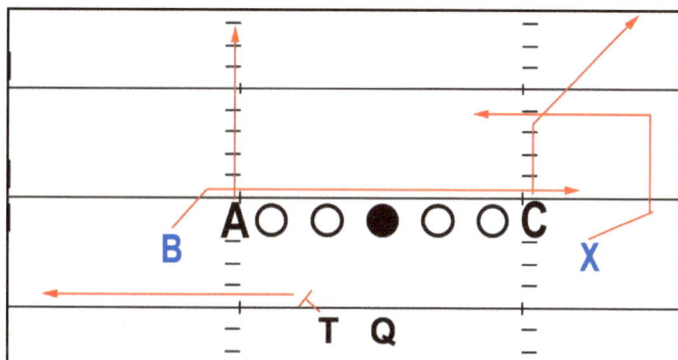

Key Points:

- Same image with 2 route changes: X-Ray runs a 29/5 (3-step slant out + 3-step up + in at 90 degree) and Alpha runs a 9 (fly).

- Bravo's 15 pattern sprints beneath two clearing routes.

- The double wing squeezes the spread without changing the image.

Example #7 same image, opposite side

Starting formation: Quick Gun Bravo 5

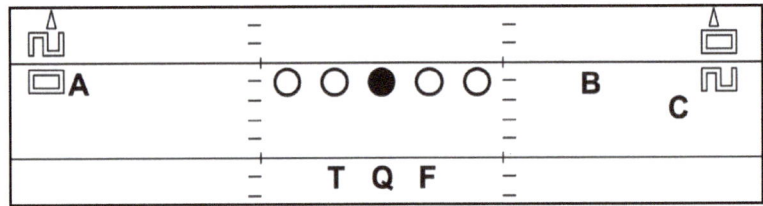

1st move: Lima 3   **2nd move: Mike 56**

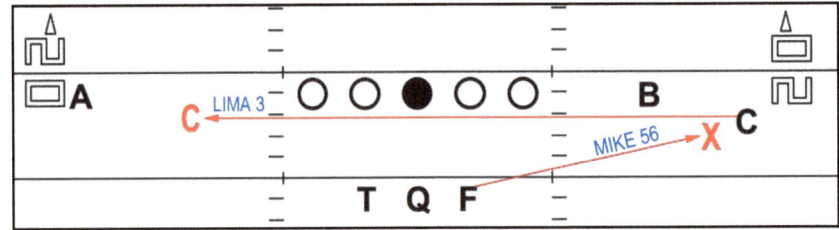

Make the Call: Alpha Charlie 95-8; 17, 15, zero

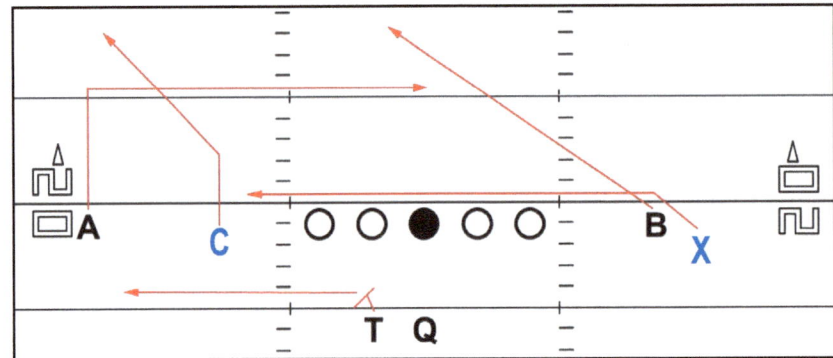

Key Points:

- Unbalanced 2x2.
- Bravo and X-ray are bunched.
- X runs low cross under Bravo's clearing.
- Charlie smashes from the inside receiver spot.
- X-Ray's 15 pattern sprints beneath two clearing routes.
- Counting the TB, four receivers are on the frontside at 4 levels.
- The TB's flare and Xs low cross are sufficiently separated.

Chapter 6: Derivative Bass Stretch Pass Diagrams

Diagram 6.1

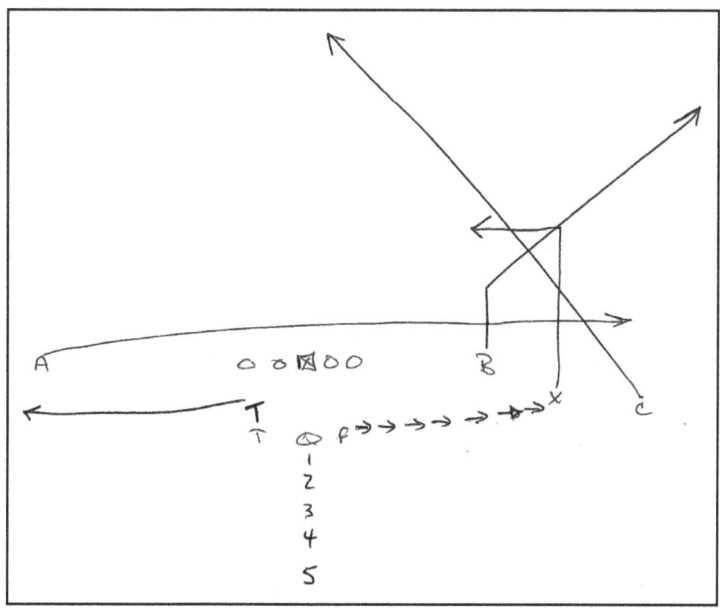

Formation: Quick Gun Bravo 5

Shift-Motion: Mike 56

FS: Bravo X-Ray 8-95

BS: 15-17-Zero

Theory: The flex formation moves the TE outside the box for an easy read and positions TE in open space. Motion creates a 1x3 semi-bunch. The trips side does not create a tight bunch but creates a partial bind.

FS: #3 and #2 build the corner-in FS farther and tighter than usual.

BS: The middle is attacked from the trip side. The flat is attacked from the single-receiver side. #1s on both sides.

Diagram 6.2

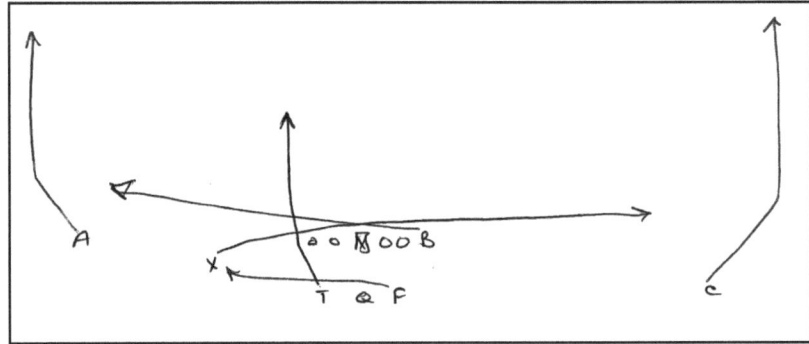

Formation: Quick Gun Bravo 5

Shift-Motion: Mike 4 Lima 45

FS: X-Ray Charlie 8-95

BS: 15-17-Zero

Theory: Tighter trips, closer to QB. More room for YAC on wide side. 1x3 closer to ball. FS built by #3 /#2. BS built by #1s on both sides.

Diagram 6.3

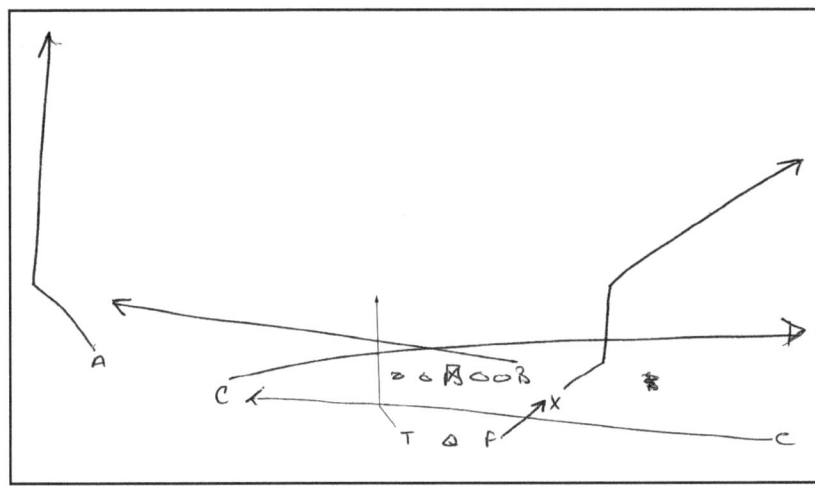

Formation: Quick Gun Bravo 5

Shift-Motion: Mike 3 Lima 4

FS: Charlie Bravo 8-95

BS: 17 – 15 – Zero

Theory: Unbalanced 2x2. Binds coverage by using one WR and one FB as H-Backs – the IR Bind... how to cover double H-Back with TE wide.

Diagram 6.4

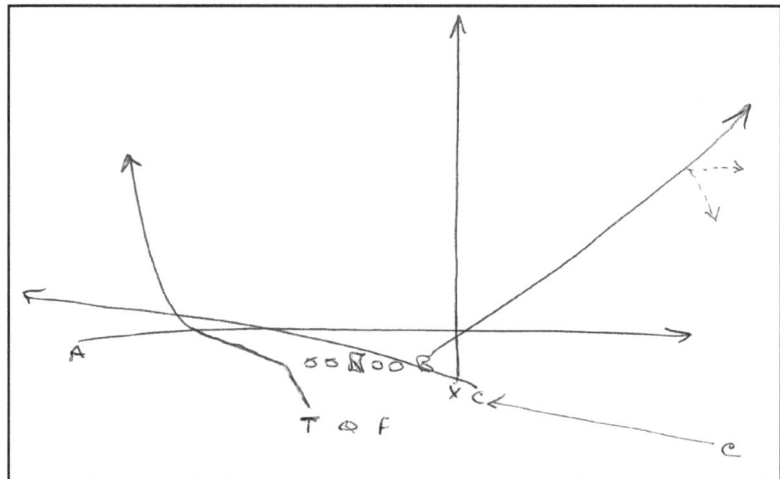

Formation: Quick Gun Bravo 5

Shift-Motion: Delta 12 Lima 2

FS: Tango Charlie 95-8

BS: 17-15-Zero

Theory: Attack middle through the FS. #1s on both sides create the BS.

Diagram 6.5

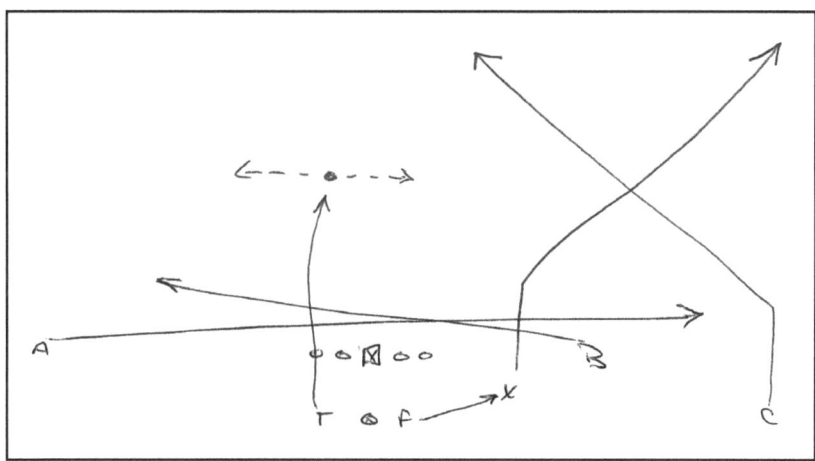

Formation: Quick Gun Bravo 5

Shift-Motion: Mike 56 Lima 12

FS: Alpha Charlie 95-7

BS: 17-15-Zero

Theory: Unbalanced 2x2. Two half bunches spread away from the ball.

Diagram 6.6

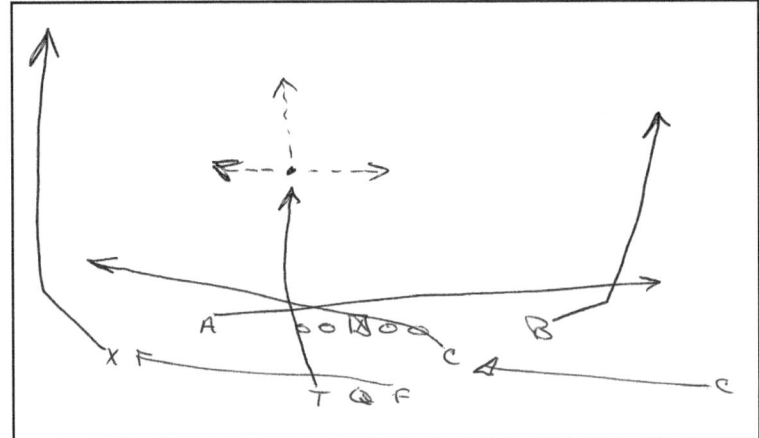

Formation: Quick Gun Bravo 4

Shift-Motion: Mike 2

FS: X-Ray Charlie 8-95

BS: 17-26-Zero

Theory: 1x3. TE with wing – essentially a Double TE on same side. 26 pattern is a spreed out – same effect as 15 – 1/2 15 – half of the shallow cross.

Diagram 6.7

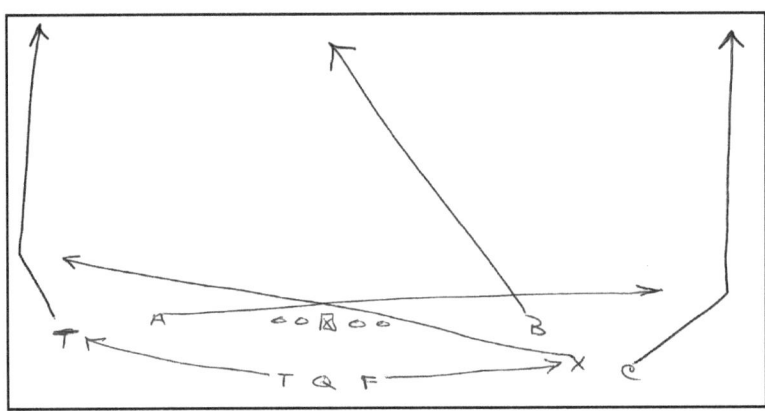

Formation: Quick Gun Bravo 4

Shift-Motion: Mike 3 Lime 23

FS: Charlie X-Ray 95-8

BS: 7-15-Zero

Theory: Unbalanced 3x1: 1/2 bunch at the IR spot. Depending on personnel, can use 1, 2 or 3 tight ends (big ends).

Diagram 6.8

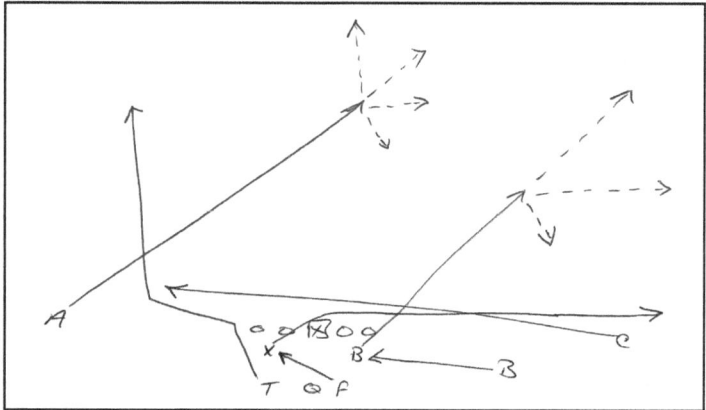

Formation: Quick Gun Bravo 4

Shift-Motion: Lima 43 Mike 45

FS: Bravo X-Ray 8-19.5

BS: 17-26-Zero

Theory: Unconventional, unbalanced 1x3. #1 is X, a WR or Big End. #3 is a hidden WR – concealed in "B"gap. Binds the defense. X 19.5 delays and positions the IN route from the B/X half bunch.

Diagram 6.9

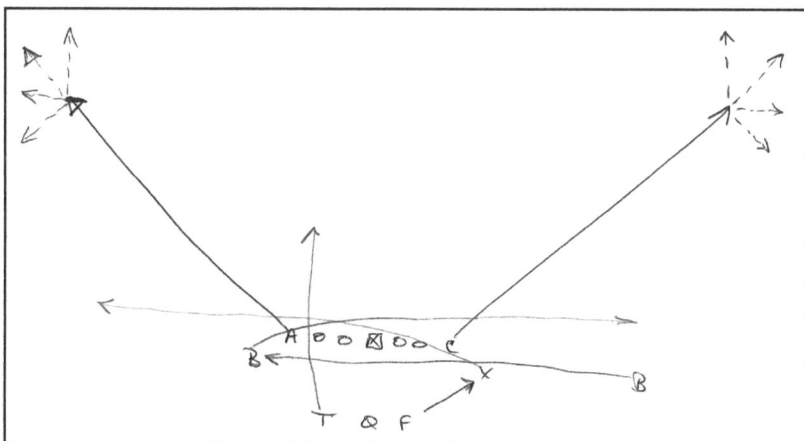

Formation: Quick Gun AC

Shift-Motion: Mike 1 Lima 2

FS: Alpha Bravo 95-8

BS: 17-15-Zero

Theory: Unbalanced 3x1. 1/2 bunch wide #1 WR becomes #2. #1 WR attacks middle of field from wide #1.

Diagram 6.10

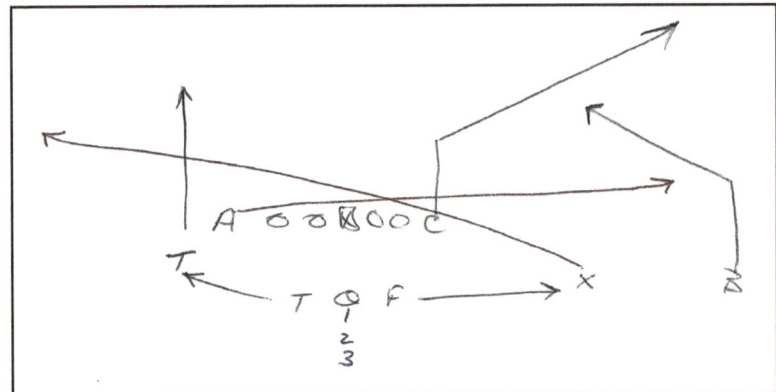

Formation: Quick Gun AC
Shift-Motion: Lima 34 Mike 4
FS: X-Ray Charlie 8-95
BS: 17-15-Zero
Theory: Unconventional, unbalanced 2x2. TE hides in B gap.

Diagram 6.11

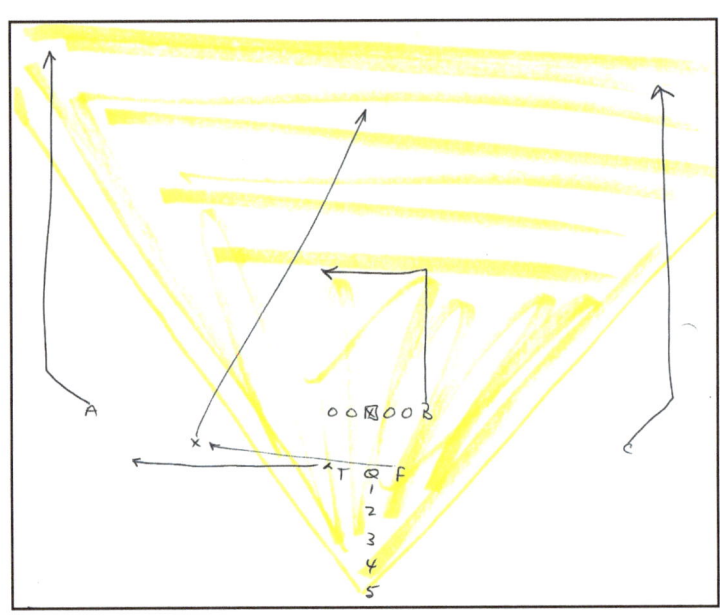

Formation: Quick Gun AC
Shift-Motion: Mike 34 Lima 3
FS: Alpha X-Ray 95-8
BS: 26-17-Zero
Theory: Unconventional, unbalanced 3x1; #3 is hidden in the box. #1 and 3 FS creates a bind.

Diagram 6.12

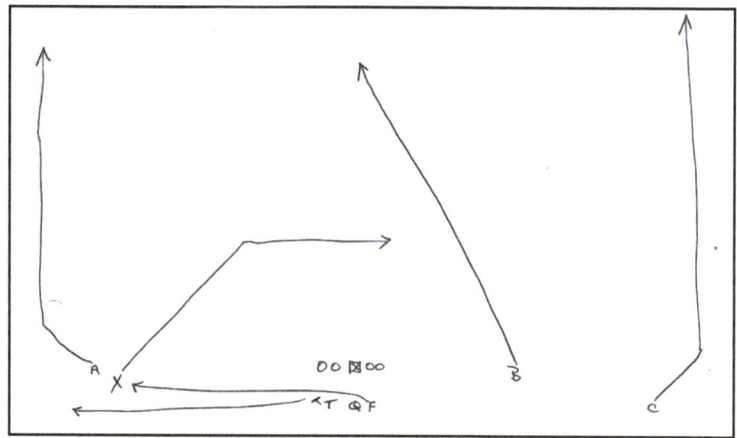

Formation: Quick Gun Alpha Bravo 25 (Double-Flex)

Shift-Motion: Mike 1 Lima 3

FS: X-Ray Charlie 95-8

BS: 17-15-Zero

Theory: Double-Flex converted to evenly-spaced 3x1. FB shifts to #1. #1 flexes at #2. #1 right side becomes #3 tripside, leaving the single-receiver side flexed. #1 and #3 trip-side from the FS. #2 trips attacks middle.

Diagram 6.13

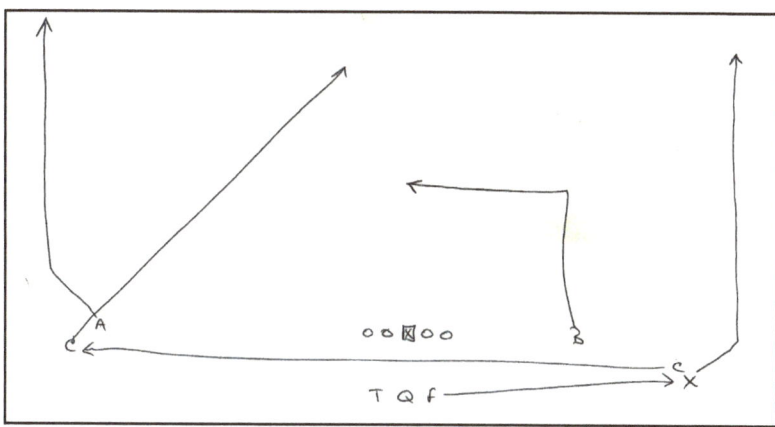

Formation: Quick Gun AC 34 (WR /2PT stand at TE) – #1 WR align tight with TE flexed

Shift-Motion: Mike 2

FS: Charlie Bravo 8-95

BS: 17-15-Zero

Theory: Unconventional tight formation resembling double TE but uses WR at TE in 2-point stance, resulting in major defensive bind. Shift converts to double flex where big ends are #2, small ends #2.

Diagram 6.14

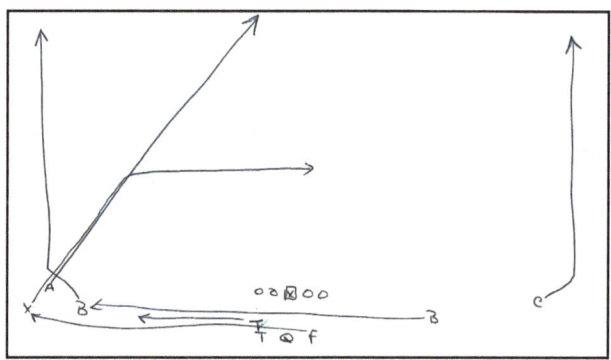

Formation: Quick Gun AC 34

Shift-Motion: Mike 4

FS: Charlie Bravo 8-95

BS: 17-26-Zero

Theory: Most unconventional 1x3. #3 (small WR) runs corner – major bind.

Diagram 6.15

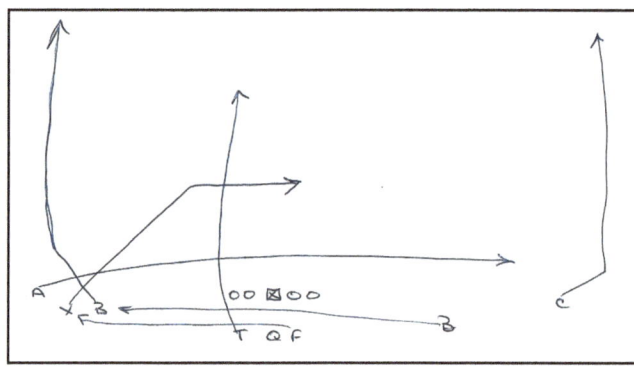

Diagram 6.16

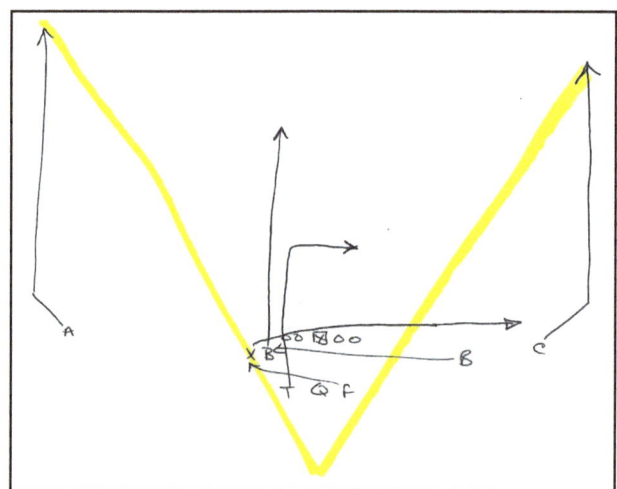

Diagram 6.17

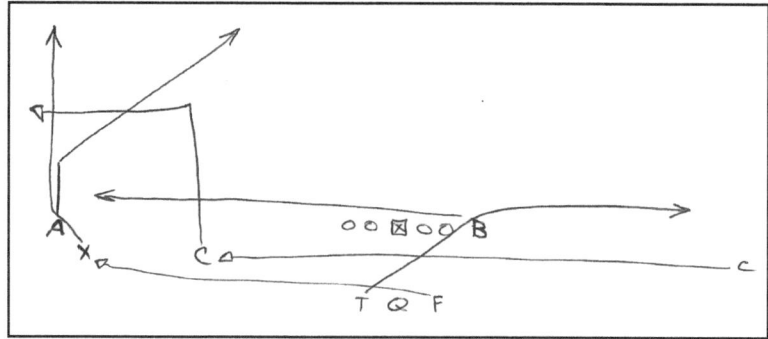

Diagram 6.18

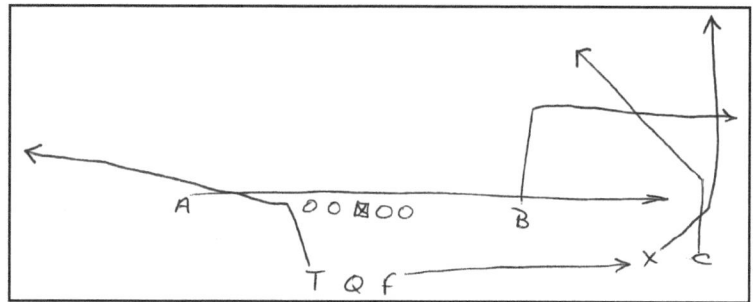

Diagram 6.19

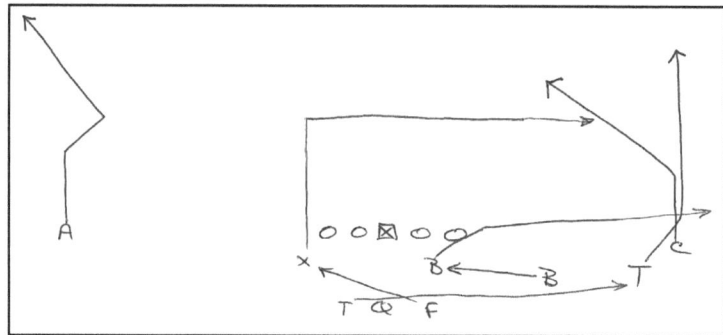

Diagram 6.20

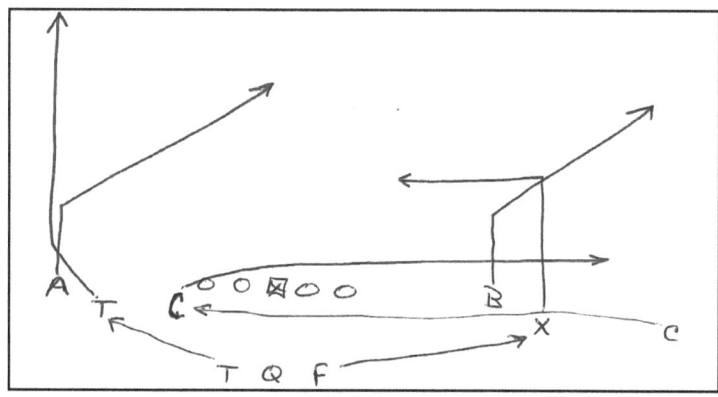

Diagram 6.21

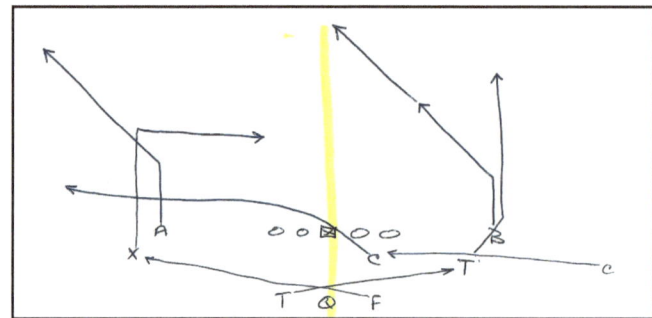

Diagram 6.22

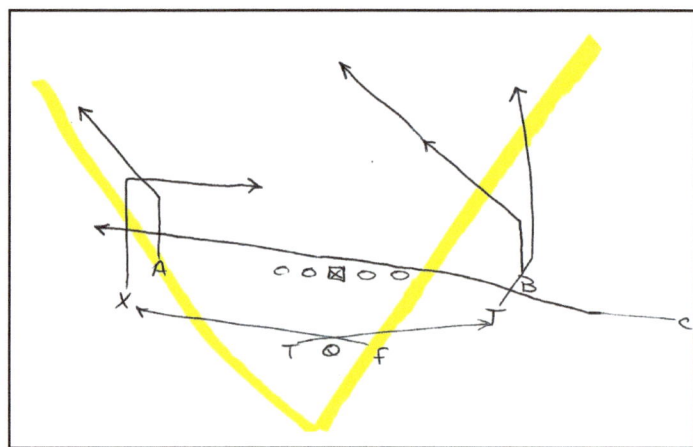

Diagram 6.23

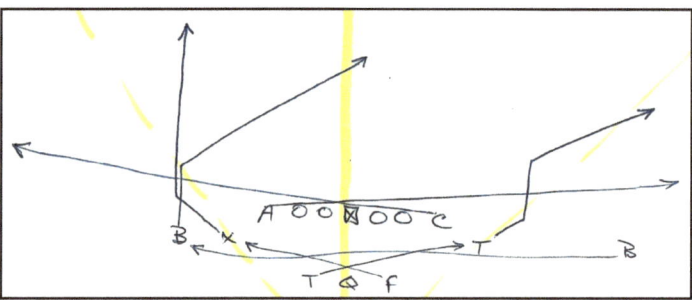

Diagram 6.24

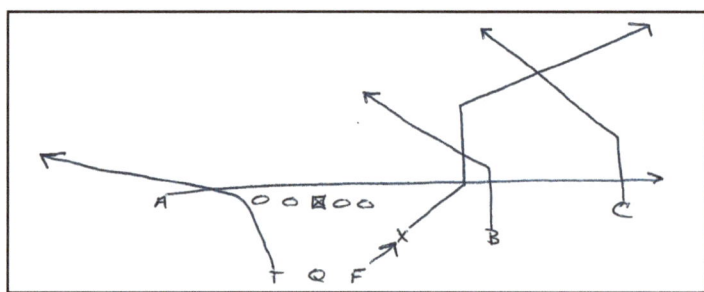

SWAT No-Huddle Offense

Diagram 6.25

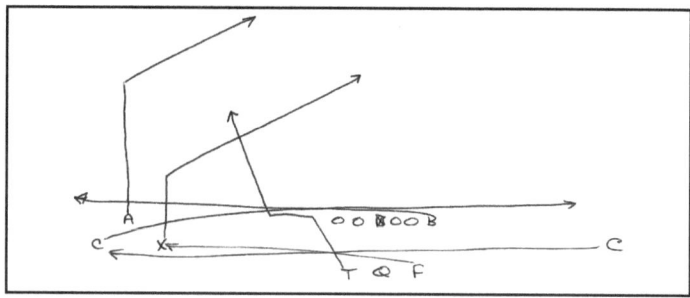

Diagram 6.26

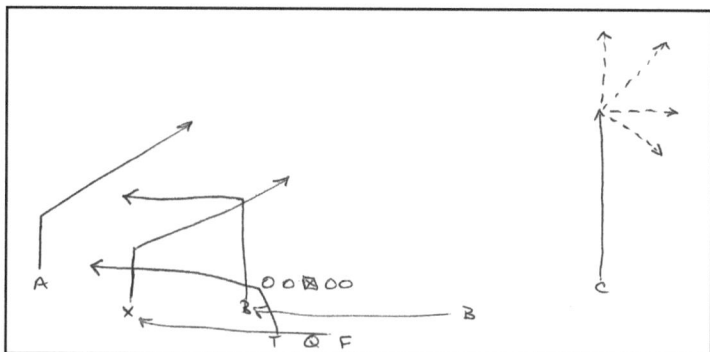

Diagram 6.27

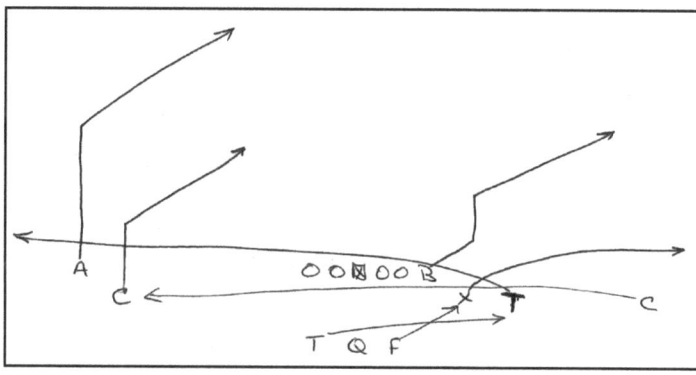

Diagram 6.28

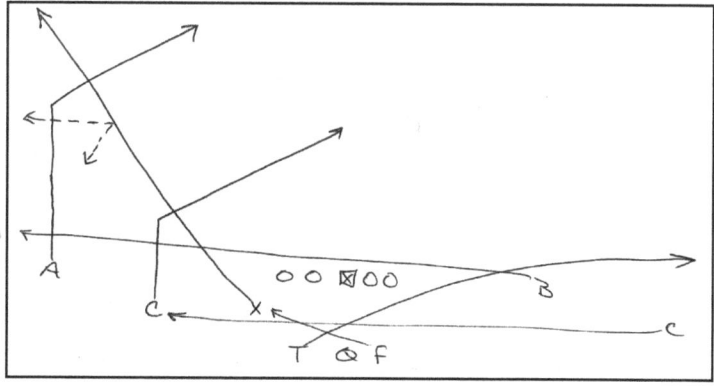

Diagram 6.29

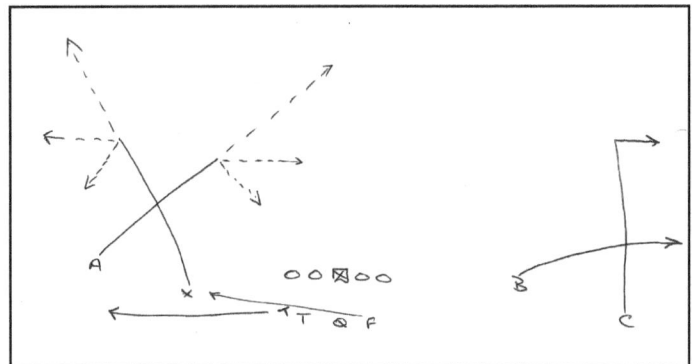

Diagram 6.30

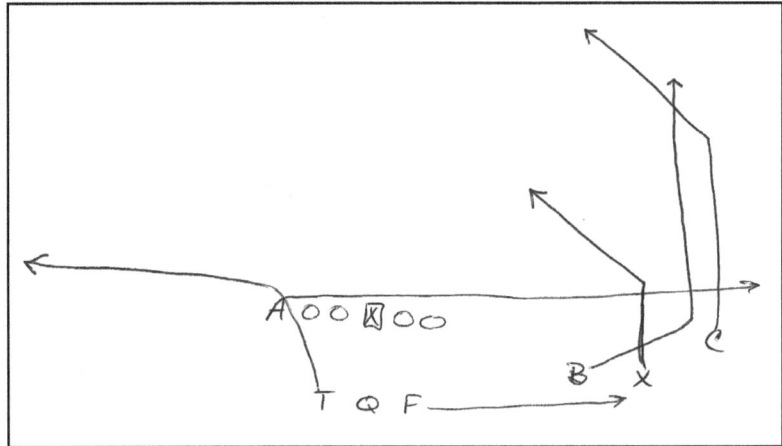

Chapter 7: Secondary Stretch Pass

Stretch Passes are a part of the SWAT system but they are not the entire system. It's my primary teaching and strategic focus. The entire strategic offense depends on learning and repping Stretch Passes first.

Stretch Passes are the deep game. They challenge the defense vertically and horizontally, forcing the defense to lose focus of the box and focusing instead on the biggest area of the football field – outside the box. Stretch passes force the defense to establish a primary to every square inch of the football field outside the clutter of the box. We have to de-clutter the box because of a fact that needs repeating – we play against a higher level of competition. We are trying to get to the point where we can out-muscle defenders in the box. We have a natural developmental process… a slow one without steroids that has to be built one rep at a time by players who have not evolved as fast as other players. Consequently, I have two strategic objectives:

1. We will out-muscle you when our second-chance players eventually pass you in the weight room.
2. But until them, we have to weaken you by tiring you out and de-cluttering the box.

Our running game and short passes are both major elements of the SWAT system but my personal research has discovered 2 rules that have worked for us:

(a) Running and short passes are connected. Short passes are an extension of the running game.
(b) Running and short passes are included in the Stretch Pass system.

I learned the concept of 'included' at police college while learning the concept of 'included offences.' Assault is an included offense with Assault with a Weapon. Here's the relevance to the SWAT system – if you learn to go deep, you have learned the basics of going short. Going short is included in the deep game. That includes the running game. This theory challenges conventional wisdom but it has worked for us. Our running game and short passing game are far easier to teach and learn because I believe run blocking is an extension of pass blocking, not vice-versa. Our pass-blocking skills and run-blocking skills are not separate – they're connected. They form a continuum. After a player becomes a pass blocker in our system, he has already learned a portion of run blocking.

Top 20 Partial Concepts

This chapter shows the next phase (#2) of our limitless pass system. Phase 2 is called Secondary Stretch Passes. These pass plays are defined as Stretch Passes built by connecting 18 more relevant partial concepts according to the 5-S model.

At the end of phase 2, we've introduced 20 total partial concepts. The first two partial concepts are the base partial concepts that connect to build the Base Stretch Pass. The next 18 are new.

The following is the total list of 20 Phase 2 partial concepts followed by diagrams that show how we connect them at the LOS using the 5-S model to form limitless Secondary Stretch Passes.

Partial Concept Name	SWAT Language
1 – Corner-In	8-95 (BASE)
2 – Double-Cross	17-15 (BASE)
3 – Double Corner – Slant and Seam	29-29
4 – Double Low Cross	15-15
5 – Post-In	7-5
6 – Double Post	7-7
7 – Post-Corner Xchange	7-29
8 – Deep-Slant Cross Option	17-0,28-0
9 – Vertical Xchange	19-29
10 – In-Out Cross	5-6
11 – Out-Post Cross	6-7
12 – Corner-Post Cross	8-7
13 – Double-Corner – 45-Degree	8-8
14 – Backfield Fly to Seam	3
15 – Backfield Flat to Seam	23
16 – Post-Corner	78
17 – Seam-Corner	29-8
18 – Out to Seam	69
19 – Dig	75
20 – Speed-Out to Seam	26-9

3: Double Corner – Slant and Seam   29-29

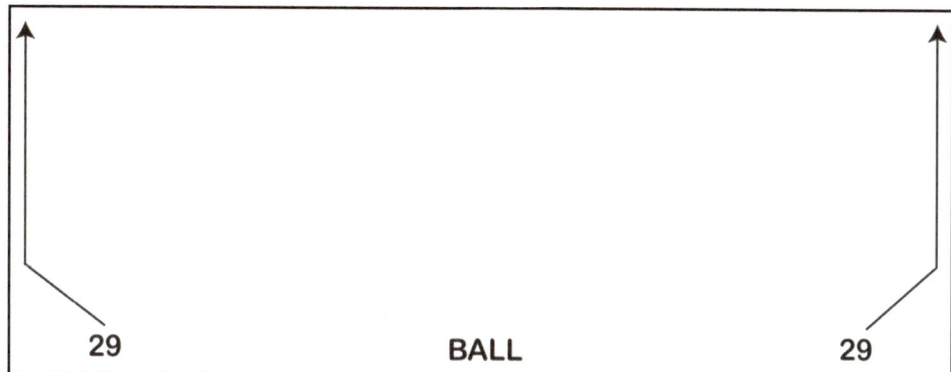

Purpose:

- Attack both deep corners of the field vertically, from opposite sides of the ball, using vertical seams instead of 45-degree-angle corner routes;
- Build the edges of a V-shape front-side;
- The 3-step slant-out is intended to avoid pressure and to widen the seam.

Key point:

- Any receiver (online or offline), #1, #2, or #3.

4: Double Low Cross — 15-15

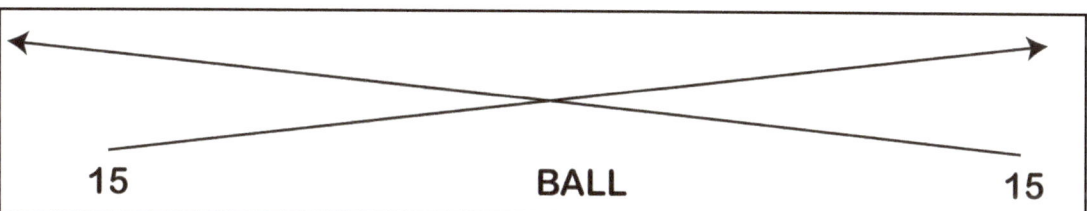

Purpose:

- Attack both flats with horizontal sprints at 30-degree angles, from opposite sides of the ball.

Key point

- Any receiver (online or offline), #1, #2, or #3, inside or outside receivers.

5. Post-In — 7-5

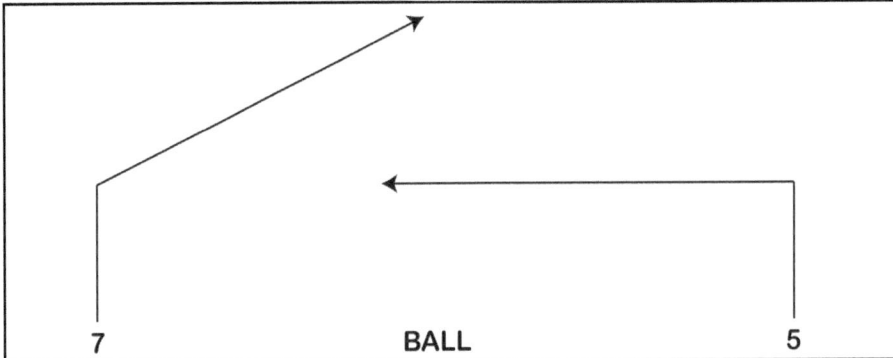

Purpose:

- Attack the midline from opposite sides of the ball, by positioning two receivers in the same sight line at 2 depth levels.

Key points:

- Any receiver (online or offline), #1, #2, or #3, inside or outside receivers.
- 5 pattern = 3-step vertical to position receiver lower. To position the him higher, change 5 to 95 pattern (6-step vertical release).
- The 7 can be changed to 97 to double the length of the vertical release.

6. Double Post — 7-7

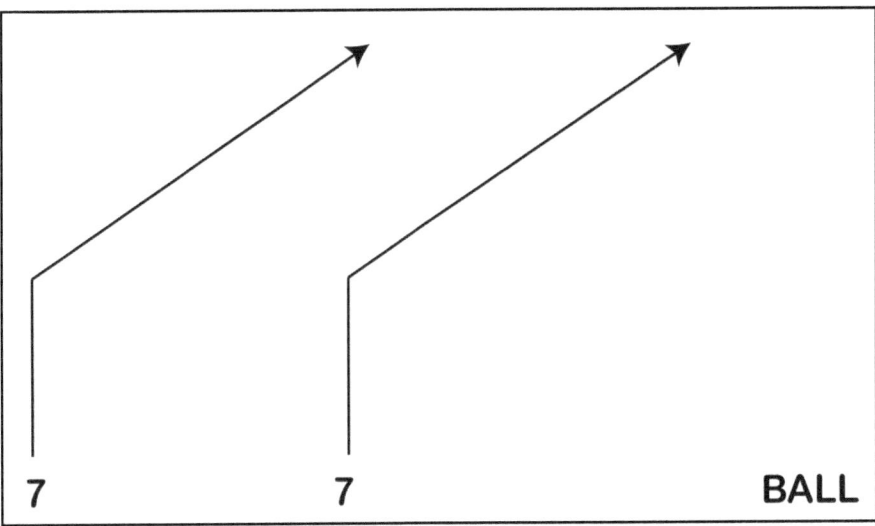

Purpose:

- Attack the edges of the deep middle from the same side of the ball, with balanced post patterns (diagram above) or unbalanced (97 and 7):

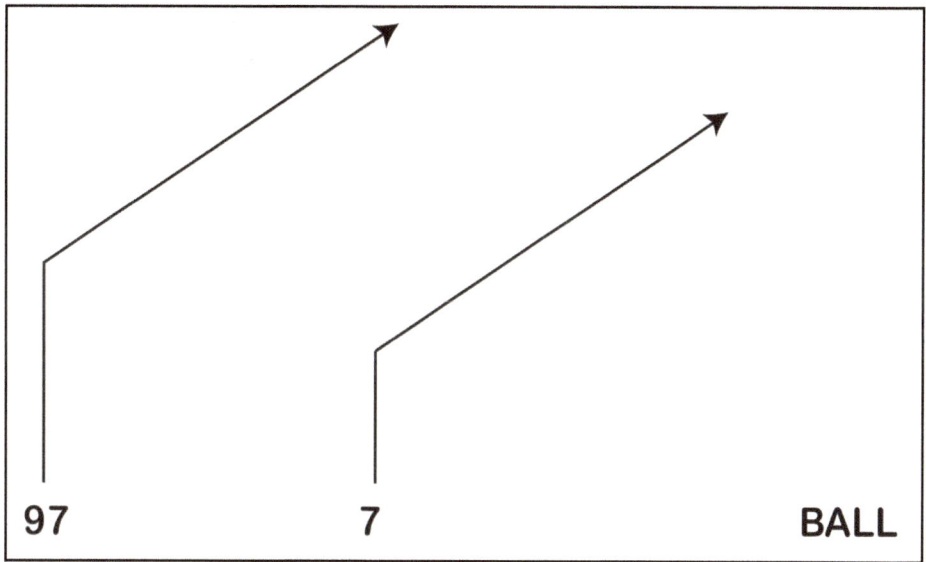

Key points:

- Any receiver (online or offline), #1, #2, or #3, inside or outside receivers.

- 7 pattern = 3-step vertical to position receiver lower. To position the him higher, add a 9 (97) pattern (6-step vertical release).

7. Post-Corner XChange — 7-29

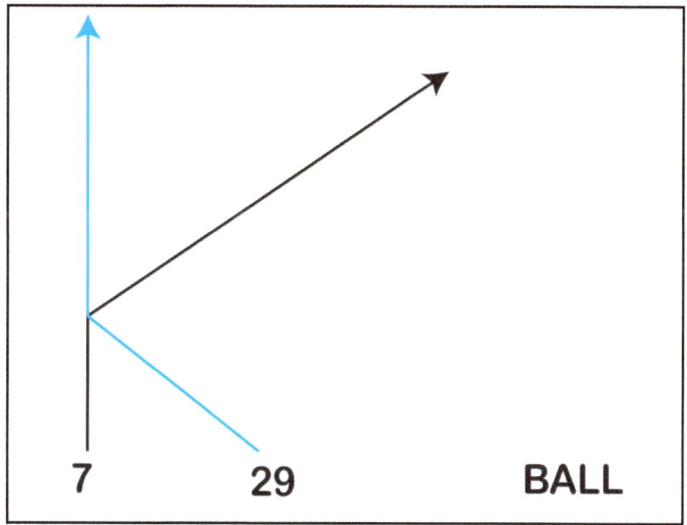

Purpose:

- Attack the post and corner from the same side of the ball, using a two-receiver lane exchange. The post pattern is the influence. The 29 pattern is the continuation of the pattern vacated by the outside receiver. The outside vertical is run like a relay – the outside receiver starts the vertical route, the inside receiver finishes it.

8. Deep-Slant Cross Option — 17-0, 28-0

(pronounced: seventeen- oh, eighteen-oh)

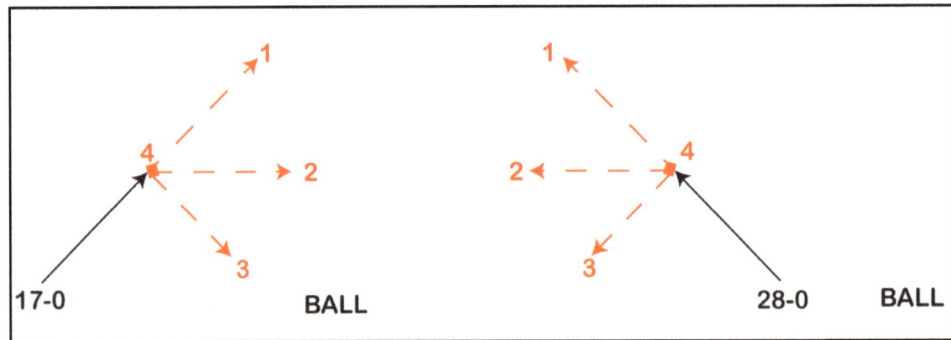

Purpose:

- Attack multiple open areas on the same side of the ball using 75-degree deep-slants, where 2-same-side receivers cross and then have discretion to make one of four calls: (i) continue on the 75-degree slant, (ii) break in/out at 90-degrees to LOS, (iii) comeback at 45-degrees, or (iv) stop.

- The decision is based on *"lane open or lane closed."* Regardless of coverage, if lane is open, stay on pattern. If closed break in/out. Stay on pattern if that lane is open. If it closes, break at 45-degrees and comeback. If every lane is closed, stop in the nearest window. This partial concept solves the problem of coverage – it works against any coverage.

9. Vertical XChange — 19-29

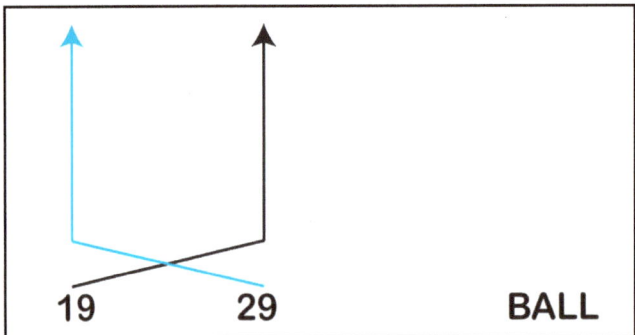

Purpose:

- Same as partial concept #8 except the cross happens immediately after release, closer to the LOS, and the receivers run vertical seams instead of slants. This partial concept attacks multiple open areas on the same side of the ball using a lane/seam change that forms an X near the LOS shortly after release. Two 45-degree slants cross to form an X, allowing receivers to exchange vertical lanes. They then have the same 4 options as described above in #8, using the *lane-open, lane-closed rule*. The five options are: (i) continue vertically, (ii) break at 45-degrees to corner or post, (iii) break at 90-degres in/out, (iv) comeback at 45-degrees, or (v) stop in nearest window.

10. In-Out Cross — 5-6

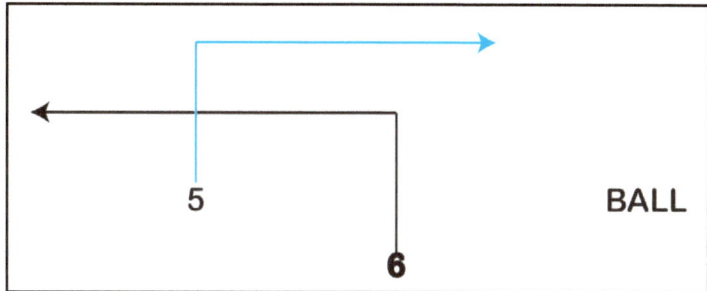

Purpose:

- Stretch the defense horizontally by executing a same-level cross on the same side of the ball to compliment vertical stretches.

11. Out-Post Cross — 6-7

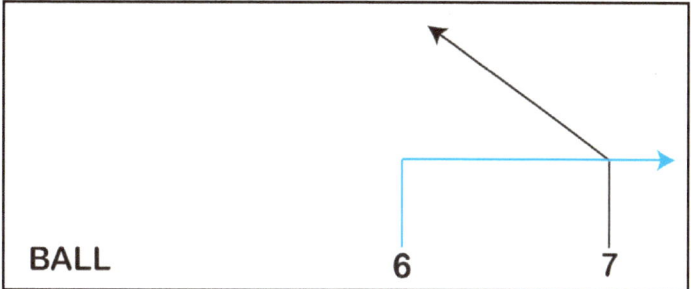

Purpose:

- Stretch the defense horizontally to the sideline and vertically to the midline by crossing 2 receivers on the same side of the ball.

12. Corner-Post Cross — 8-7

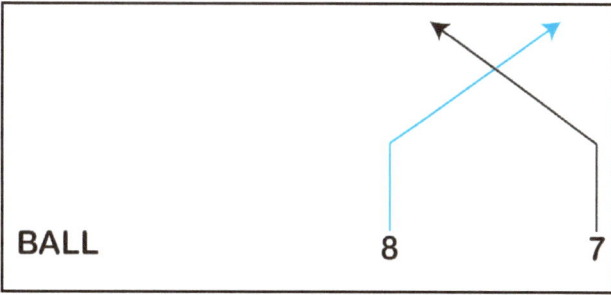

Purpose:

- Vertical stretch attacking midline and corner from 45-degree angles.

13. Double-Corner – 45-Degree — 8-8

Purpose:
- Wide vertical stretch to open the middle. Attack deep third with 45-angle routes from outside or inside receiver positions, building the borders of a V-shape frontside.

14. Backfield Fly to Seam — 3

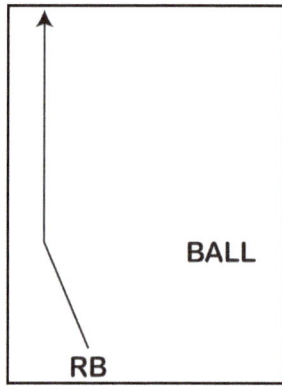

Purpose:
- Middle vertical stretch. Attack short or deep midline or exploit mismatch with LB, using a fly pattern from the backfield. Aim point = inner C gap, tackle's heel.

15. Backfield Flat to Seam — 23

23 pattern (2 = flat + 3=seam)

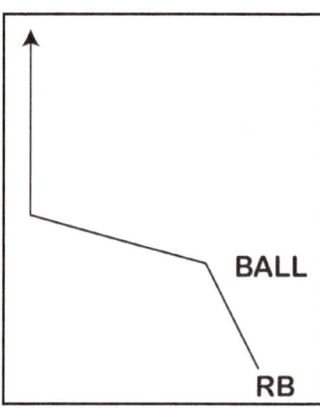

Purpose:

- Perimeter vertical stretch. Attack the low deep one-third zone through the vertical unprotected seams between low zone defenders to the vertical seam that divides short and deep zones or exploit mismatch with LB, using a longer-developing wider-fly pattern from the backfield. Aim point = inner C gap, tackle's heel.

16. Post-Corner — 78

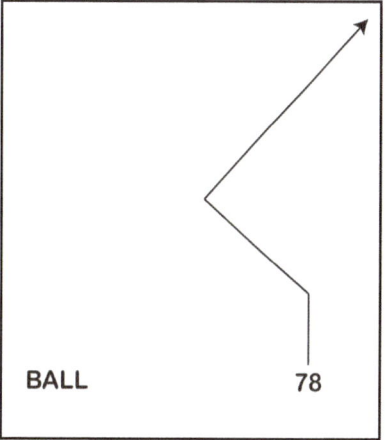

Purpose:

- Outside vertical stretch. A one-pattern concept, intended to attack deep one-third with a slow-developing 45-degree entry or exploit man coverage. Used online or offline, outside or inside receiver positions.

17. Seam-Corner — 29-8

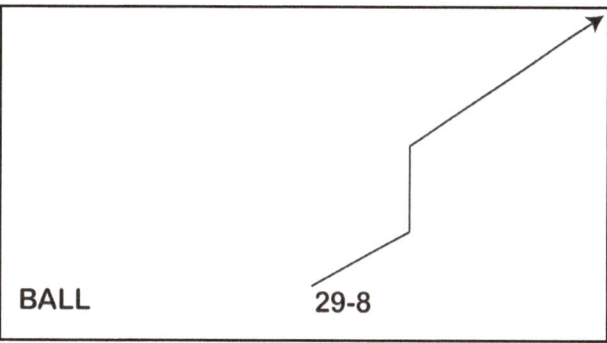

Purpose:

- Slow-developing outside vertical stretch. Used only from the inside receiver position (#3 in trips). Builds the most challenging bind for any coverage. Our longest-developing deep one-third attack, our strongest mismatch versus man cover – 100% guarantee big play capability when connected properly according to 5-S specifications.

18. Out to Seam — 69

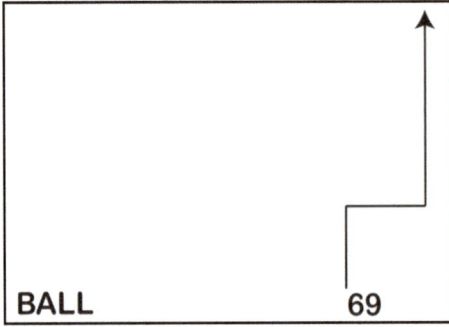

Purpose:

- Outside vertical stretch. Long-developing vertical seam intended to separate from zone or man defenders by defender's wrong footwork and angles.

19. Dig — 75

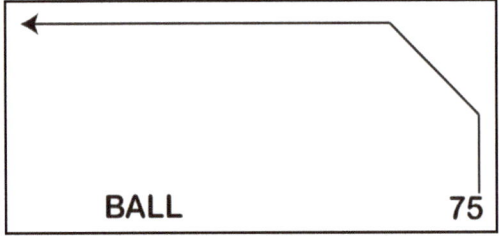

Purpose:

- Horizontal stretch. 3-step vertical release and post route versus man. 6-step vertical or post versus zone to enter the horizontal dividing seam separating deep and short zones.

20. Speed Out to Seam — 26-9

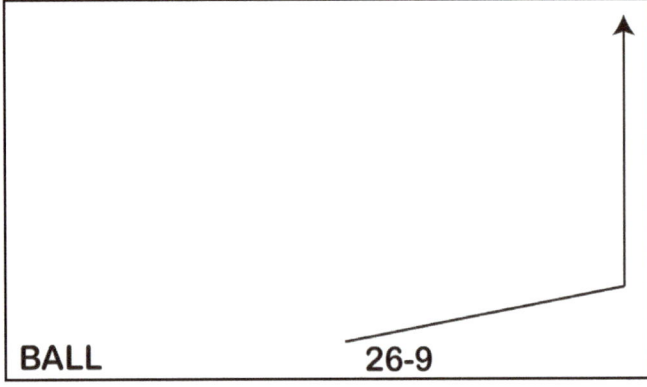

Purpose:
- Horizontal stretch followed by a vertical stretch. 2 = 3-step outside slant to the sideline. 6 = out pattern with a 3-step vertical. 26 is a speed out, combining a 2 and 6 to form the frontside of a 15 pattern (low cross). 15 and 26 have the same objective – attack the flat. 15 does it from the backside, 26 does it from the frontside. Adding a 9 to 26 builds "search" vertical seam – the inside receiver searches for the best lane while horizontally stretching along a 30-degree sprint.

Top 20 Partial Concepts — Key Points and Conclusions

The top 20 partial concepts is not the entire SWAT passing system. It's Phase 2, a manageable learning outcome based on conclusions I've reached from the evidence gathered from self-investigation. I replaced the phrase 'film study' with 'self-investigation' – change the focus, change the outcome. When I did film study, I acted like a teacher marking an essay – find fault with my team. When I changed it to self-investigation, I discovered **solutions**.

My self-investigation revealed overwhelming evidence that led to five conclusions – the top 20 partial concepts: (i) work against any coverage under intense pressure of a warp-speed no–huddle; (ii) are best for point-zero QBs and receivers to learn from; (iii) are the fastest that can be called by QBs and myself to comply with our 8-second clock; (iv) form a deep package of stretch passes, a **general game plan** that I use for any opponent, thereby solving my problem of a one-man coaching staff and not having the luxury of coaching football full-time; (v) made the biggest impact in games versus stronger competition – performance stats don't lie. Physical evidence is the strongest evidence, stronger than anecdotal statements of suspicion.

The top 20 partial concepts can connect into a limitless Secondary Stretch Pass sub-set of the limitless SWAT system. The running game and short passing game are not part of this sub-set for all the reasons mentioned previously – pedagogical and strategic. The following diagrams are some examples of how to apply the SWAT system – how to connect the top-20 partial concepts, how to communicate the call at the LOS by applying the SWAT dictionary and language.

Diagram 7.1a

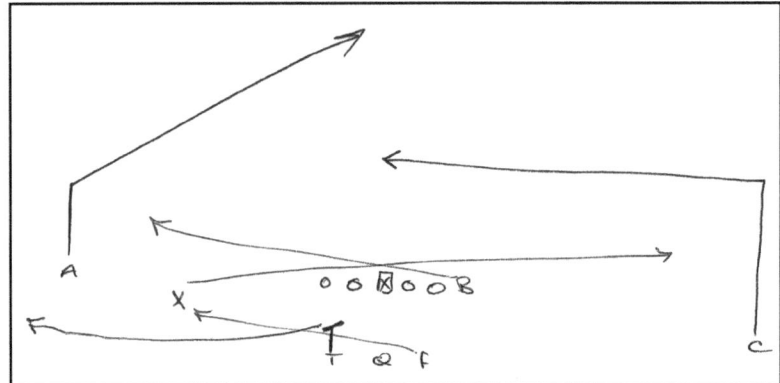

Theory:

- This play combines two partial concepts (15-15 and 7-5).
- The purpose is to stretch horizontally, vertically, and fill the void in the middle.
- Man-buster or zone-buster.
- Can be run from a number of formations.
- Versus man – the deep and intermediate middle are attacked.
- Versus Cover 1, the free safety should be occupied by the post pattern leaving 1o1 coverage on the other three receivers.
- Versus Cover 0 – there are 4 hot receivers – post, both double crosses and tailback.
- Versus Zone – three high-low binds are created. Two open horizontal seams are attacked – the dividing line between deep and shock zones (over/under lane) and the lane near the LOS beneath the short zone.
- The back attacks behind the LOS.
- Compliance with 5-S Model – separation – spacing – security.

Play-Call

- Starting formation: QGB 4.
- Final formation: Mike 2 (F-X Shift).
- Builds an unbalanced 2x2 single-back shotgun formation. WR+SB on left; TE and WR on right.
- OC Call: X-Ray Bravo 15-15.
- QB Call: 7-5-Zero (left to right, into backfield).
- Snap: first word after 3 plays + pause.
- What is the front-side? — in this case, the Right 90°-angle because X-Ray was the first digit. This front-side includes 3 Receivers (X, C, A).

Diagram 7.1b

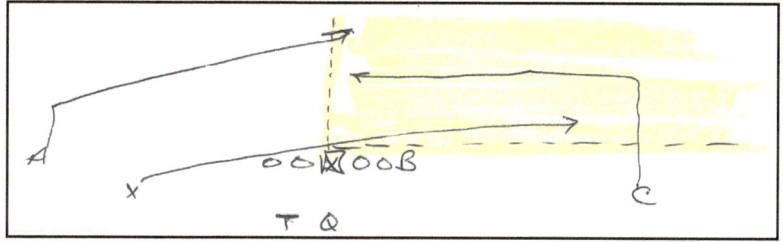

- the yellow-shaded area is the front-side

Examples:
- OC Calls: Bravo X-Ray 15-15
- QB Calls: 7-5-Zero

Diagram 7.1c

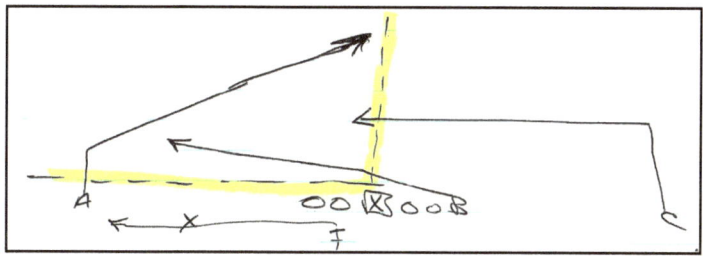

* Left 90° angle FS (4 receivers + 1BS)

OR
- OC Calls: ALPHA CHARLIE 7-5
- QB Calls: 15-15-Zero

Diagram 7.1d

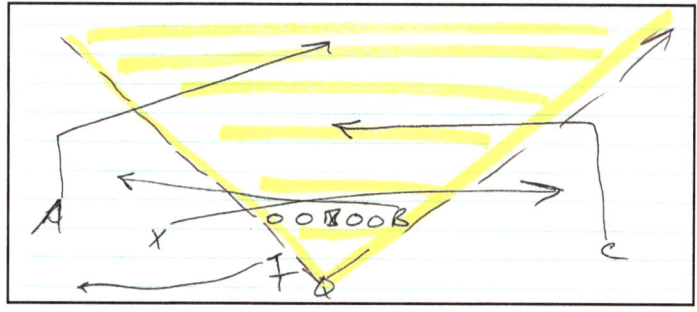

– V Shape 90° FS (middle) – 2 receivers

Summary:

- This secondary stretch pass is multi-dimensional. It can be built from various formations and can change the frontside to match the situation.
- This secondary stretch pass builds a similar image to the Base Stretch Pass. The only difference is Bravo's pattern – instead of an 8 (corner) in the base, the route changes to 15 (low cross).
- Low-Cross patterns are almost unstoppable. The two-in-one play forms one of the simplest ways to dramatically increase completion percentage, YAC and defensive fatigue. The Base Stretch Pass and the first secondary stretch pass are examples of how to form a mini-system – a system within a system.
- These two plays alone can form limitless possibilities. They can get the ball easily into the hands of all 5 receivers from wide-ranging formations without compromising.
- The 8-second clock. These two plays are 5-S compliant and teach the Board Theory of finding open receivers.
- 5-S: all receivers are separated and spaced properly. The safeties are occupied by receivers or QB's eyes.
- Hot receivers are incorporated in each play and, most importantly, receivers are grouped in "same sight lines" to form a manageable, searchable area.
- The similar downfield images are burned deeper in the QB's long-term memory, raising the QB's IQ. His Instinct Quotient raises higher and higher with each rep, letting them make the right call about receiver selection to match the situation.

Diagram 7.2

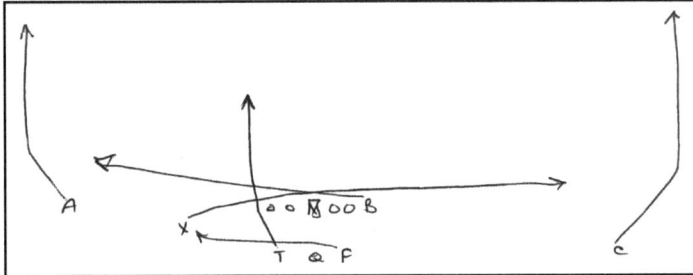

Theory:

- 2x2 balance.
- Cross low with #2s.
- Concept #3 29-29 slant out and up (attack deep outside 1/3s).
- RB flies outside tackle's heel to gap and then deep middle.

    FS = 1st letter side   **X = Right side front side**

Diagram 7.3

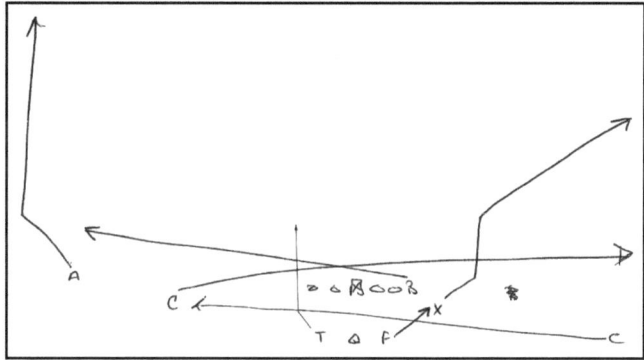

Theory:

- Unbalanced 2x2.
- 29-8 = corner with 3 paths.
- Attacks deep outside 1/3s.
- Fill void with AB (#3)Bs.

Diagram 7.4

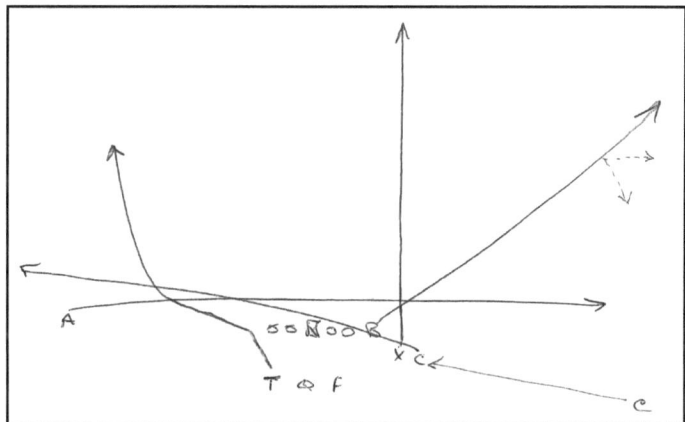

Theory:

- Unconventional tight 1x3.
- Uses #1 small ends as the double-cross.
- #3 runs 75° to corner (28) no vertical release.
- #2 attacks middle.
- RB (23) flat and fly.
- **Note:** Both 15s are hot
- If QB pressured = run.
- 5 Receiver = QB running play disguised as pass.

Diagram 7.5

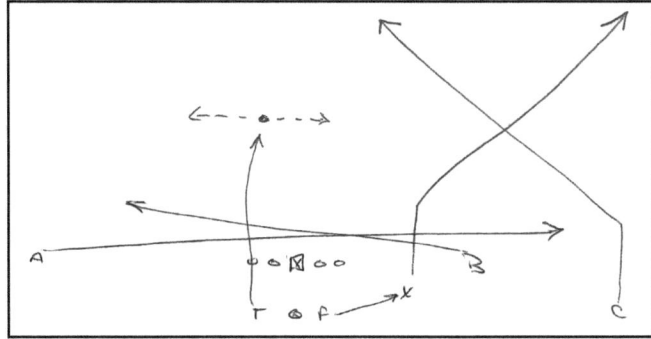

Theory:
- 1x3. #1 and #2 cross, allowing #1 and #3 trips side to cross deep.
- 3 receivers on FS in same sight line.

Diagram 7.6

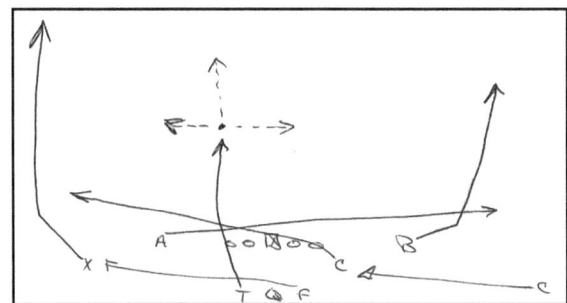

Theory:
- Unbalanced 2x2. Small WRs (A andC) are both #2s and stretch horizontally.

Diagram 7.7

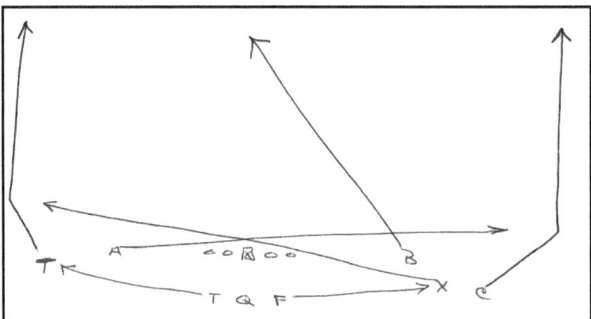

Theory:
- 2x3.
- Trips bunch. #2s on both sides cross.
- #1s stretch vertical.
- #3 trips-side attack deep middle.

Diagram 7.8

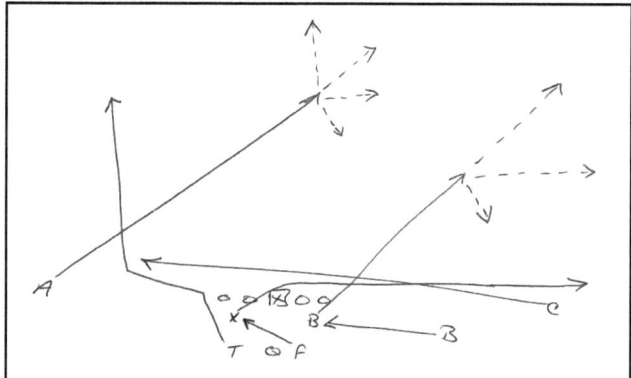

Theory:
- Unconventional 2x2.
- Wide and tight – hides both #2s in B-gaps.
- #2 and #1 cross.
- 3 Deep 1/3s are attached.
- Reminder of detours.

Diagram 7.9

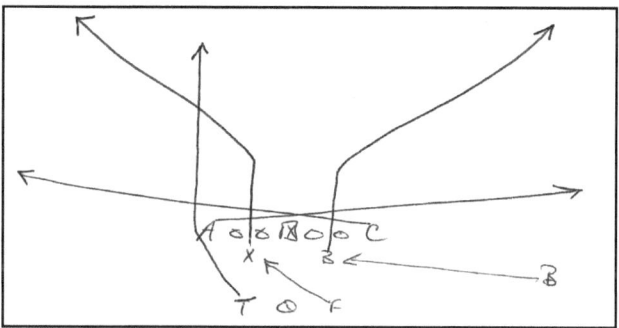

Theory:
- Tight formation.
- 2x2 balanced, all within the box.
- #2s are hidden.
- #1s cross.
- #2 sprint to corner.
- RB attacks middle.

Diagram 7.10

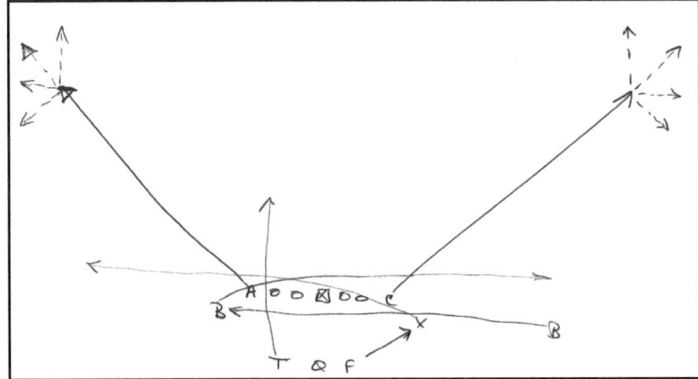

Theory:

- A derivative of 2x2 tight – double-wind. Re-positions #2 to #1. #1s cross, #2s smash.

Diagram 7.11

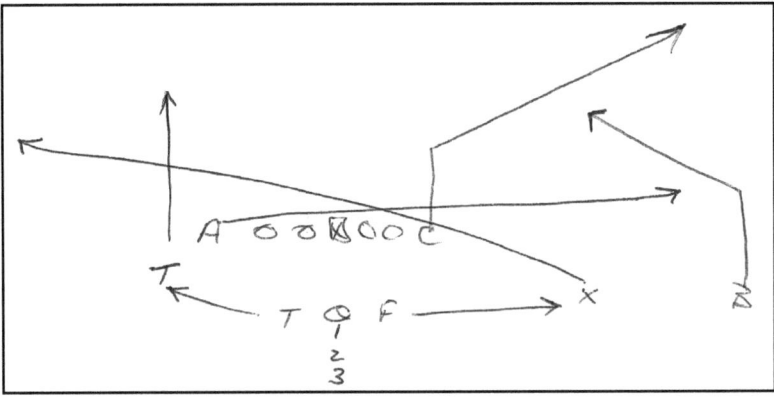

Theory:

- AX Facilitates the crossing – chose to the other side.
- QB has 3-step discretion on all empty formation.
- #2s cross, creating the best defensive bind regardless of coverage.
- 3 high/low binds are built.

Diagram 7.12

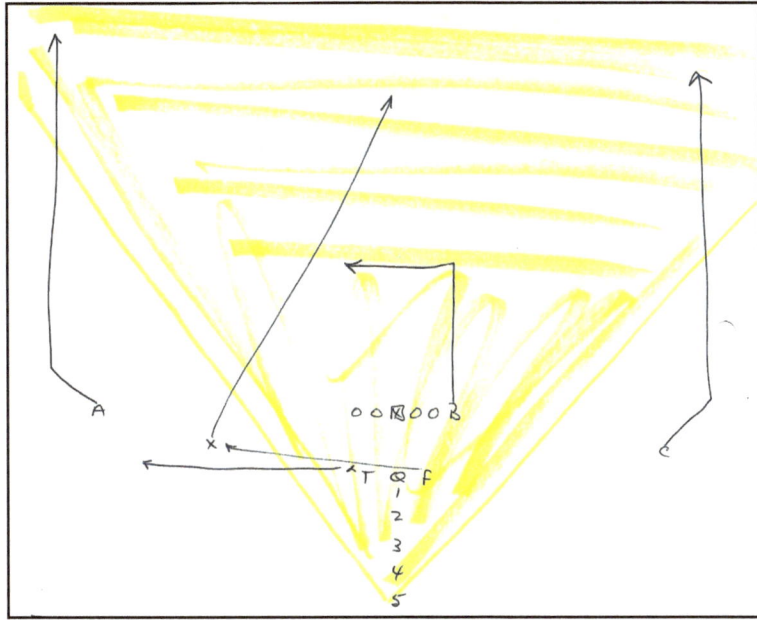

Diagram 7.13

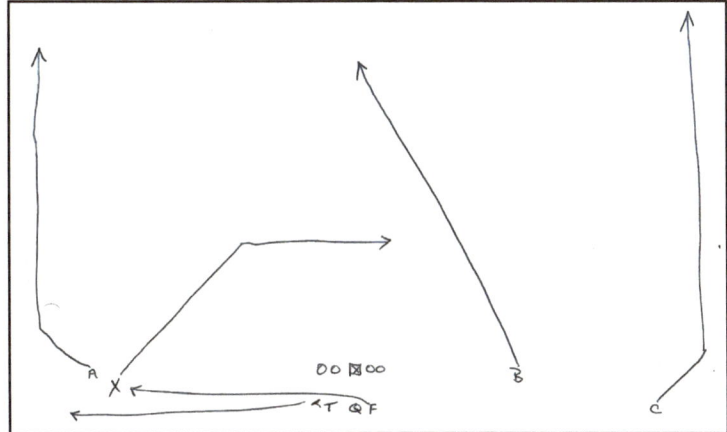

Diagram 7.14

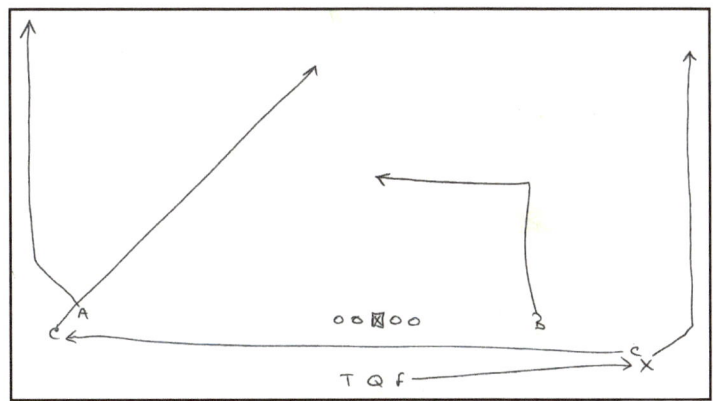

Diagram 7.15

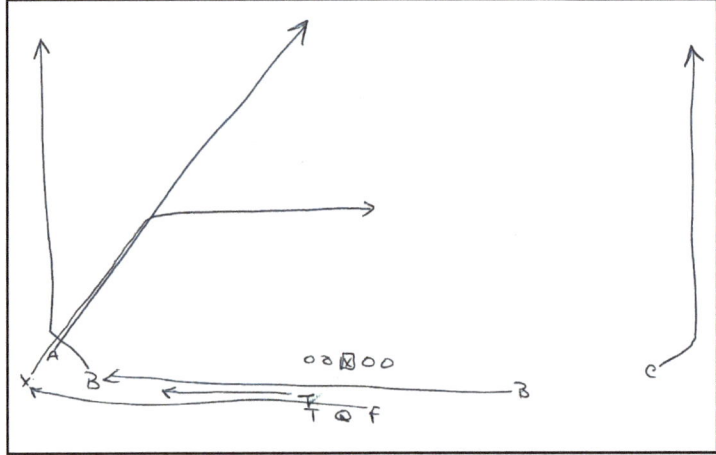

Diagram 7.16

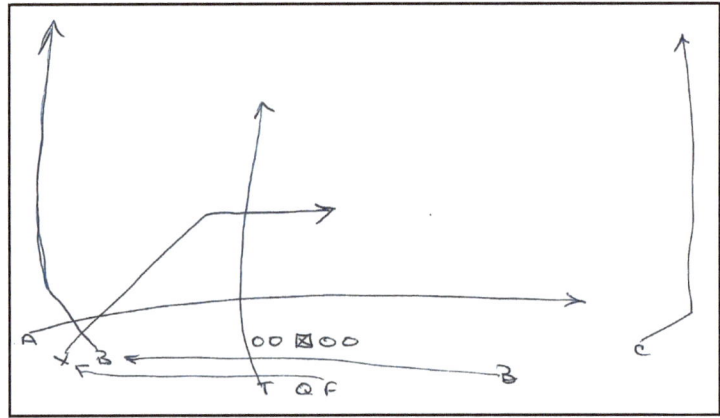

Diagram 7.17

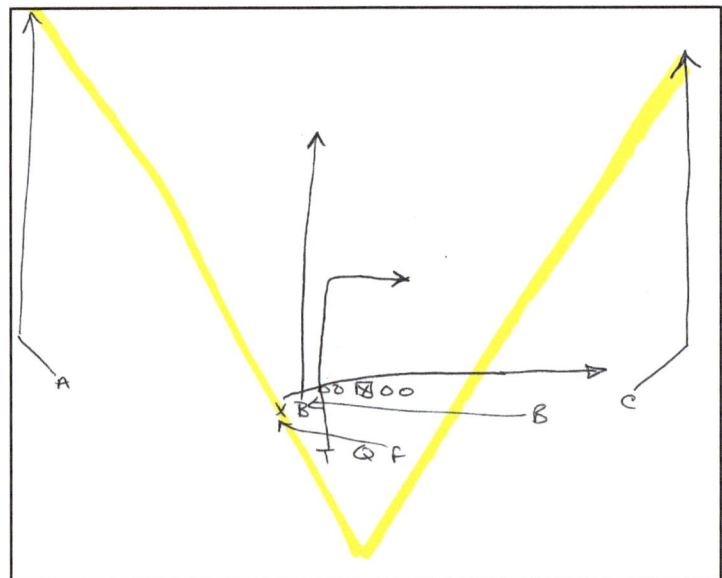

Diagram 7.18

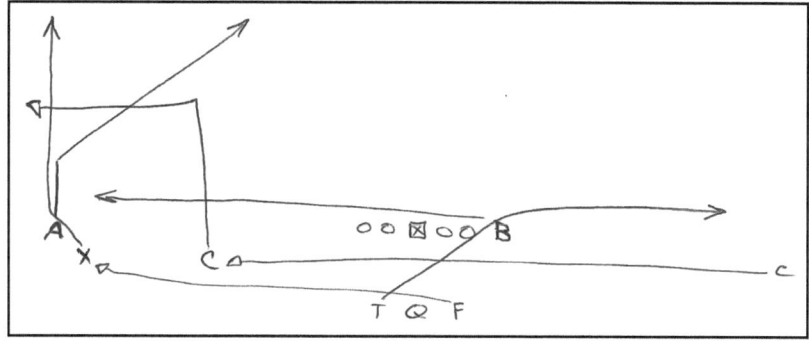

Diagram 7.19

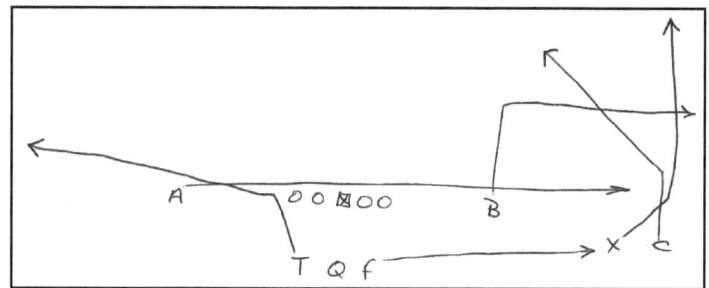

Diagram 7.20

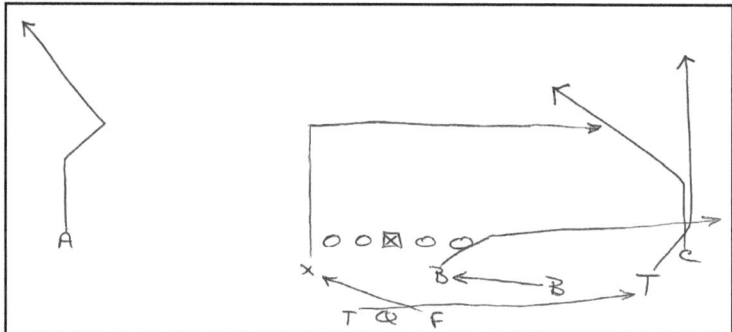

Diagram 7.21

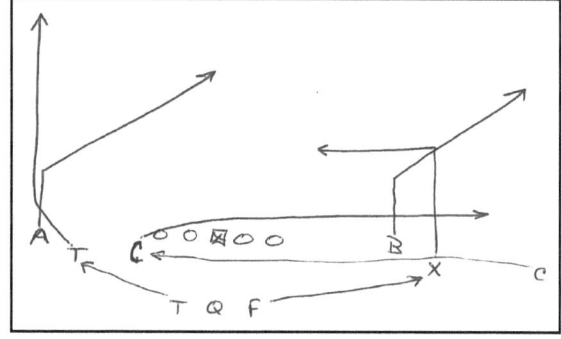

Diagram 7.22

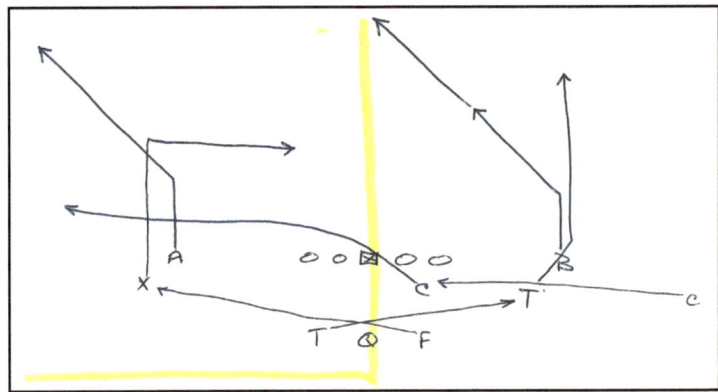

Diagram 7.23

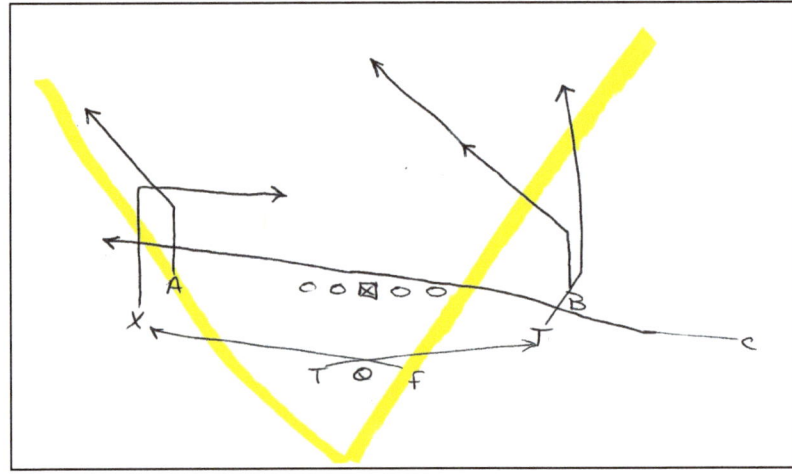

Diagram 7.24

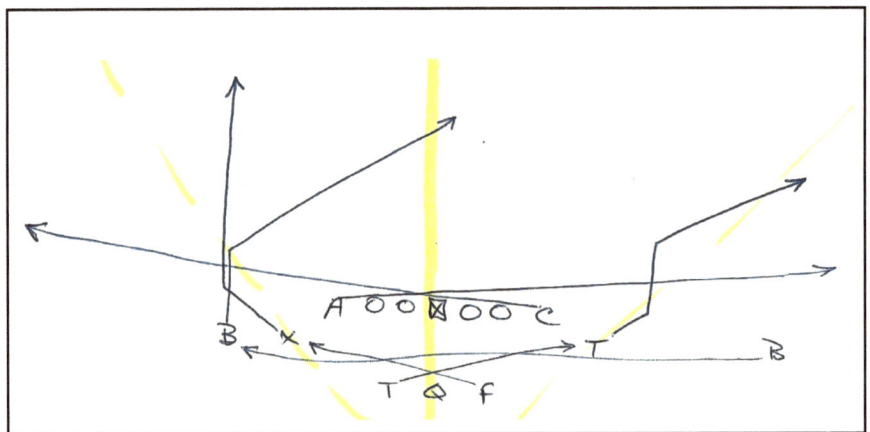

Diagram 7.25

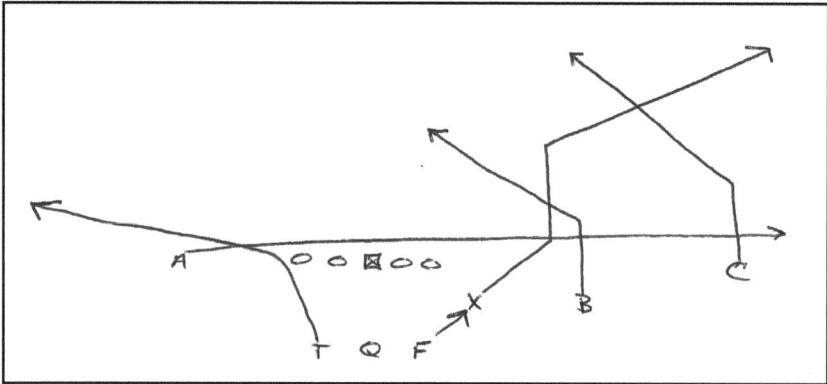

Diagram 7.26

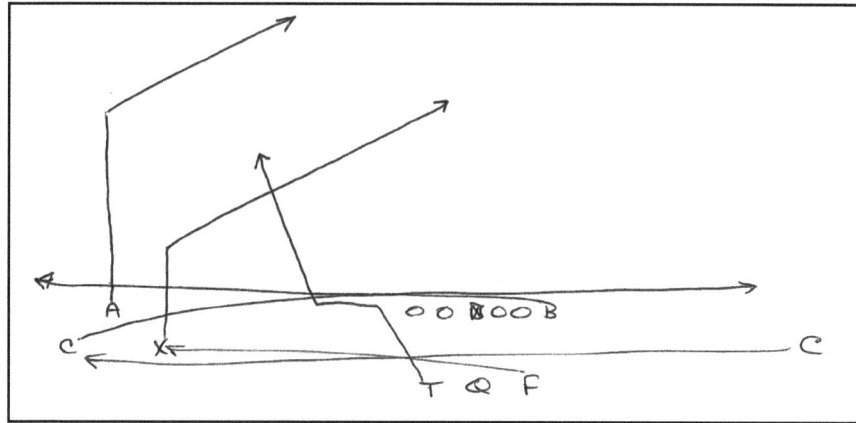

Diagram 7.27

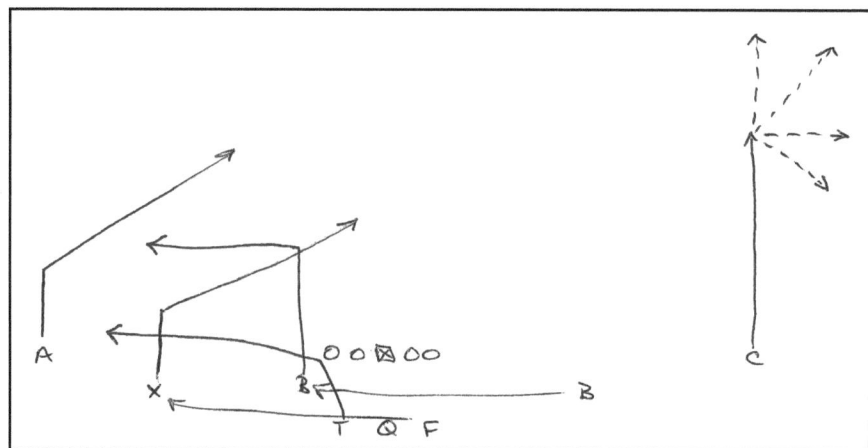

Diagram 7.28

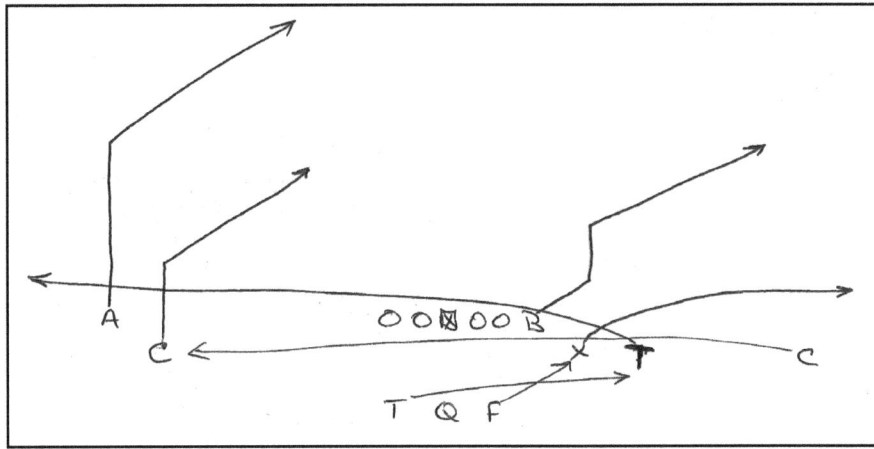

Diagram 7.29

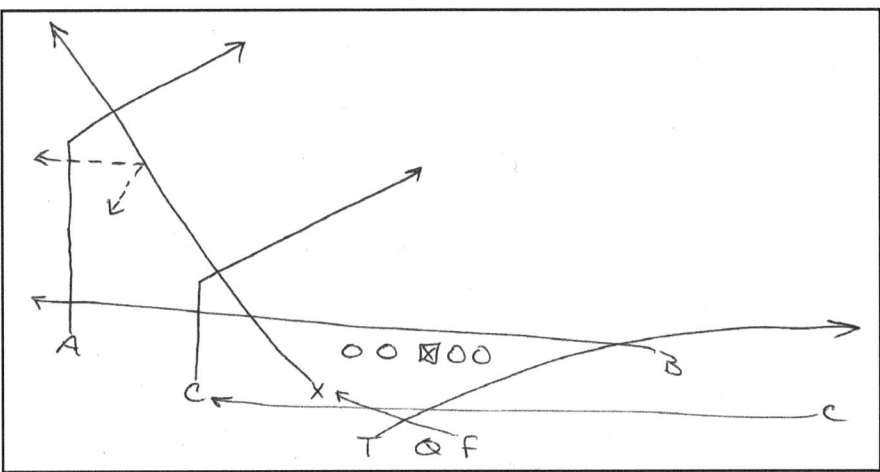

Diagram 7.30

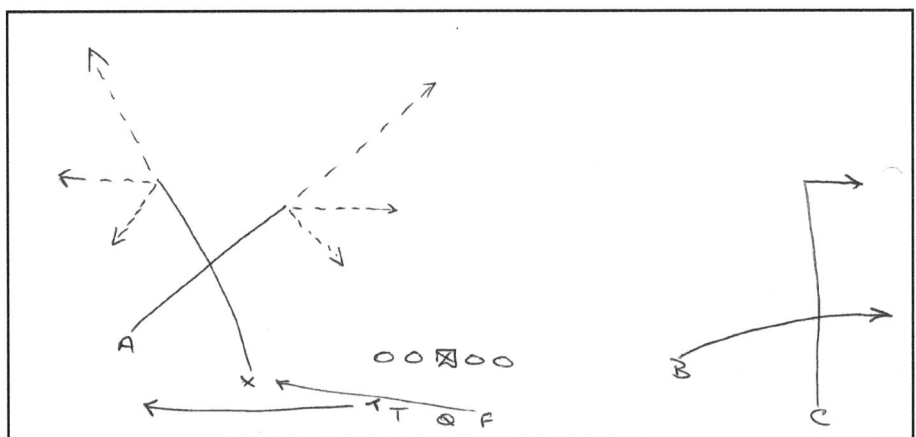

Diagram 7.31

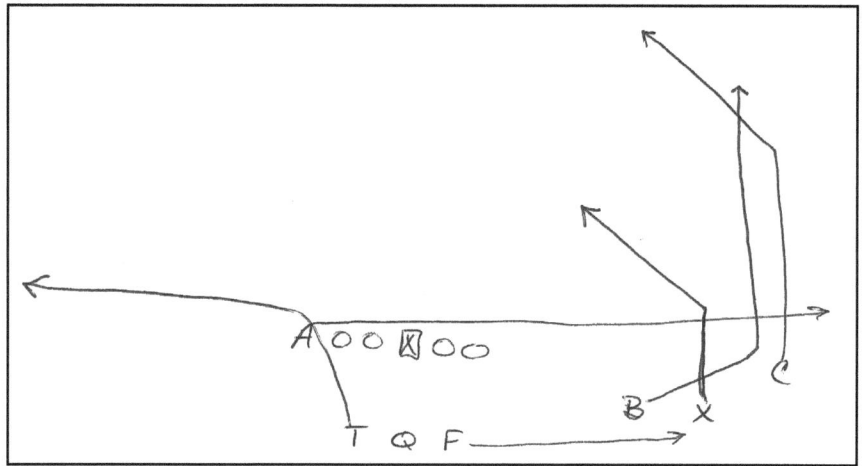

Diagram 7.32

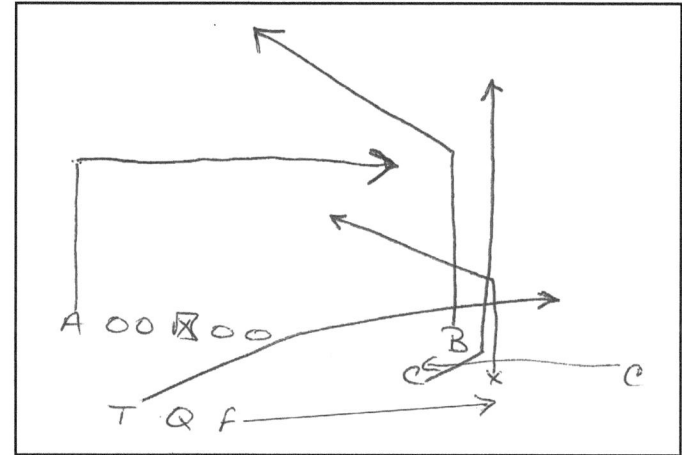

Diagram 7.33

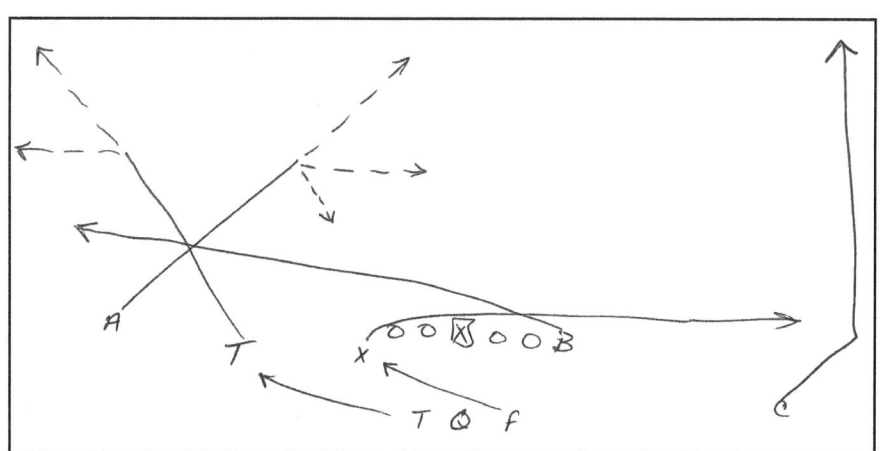

Diagram 7.34

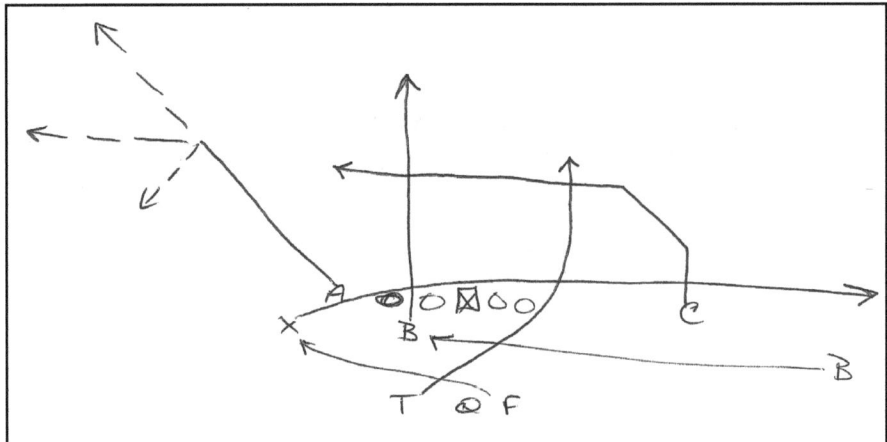

Diagram 7.35

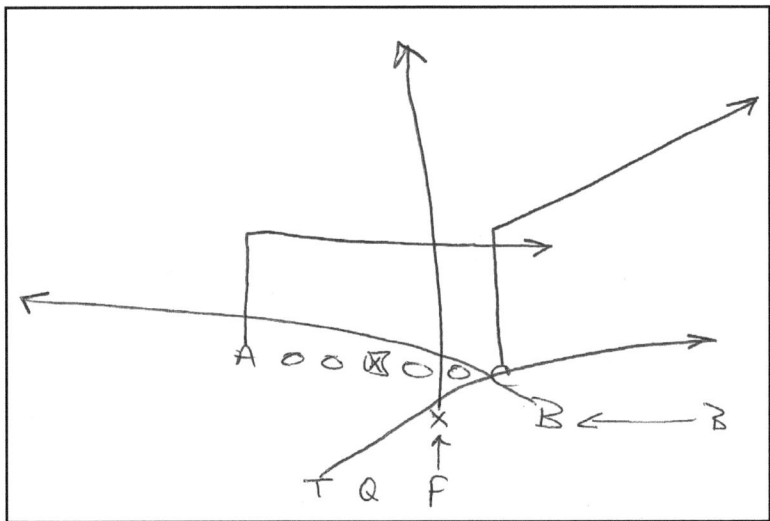

Diagram 7.36

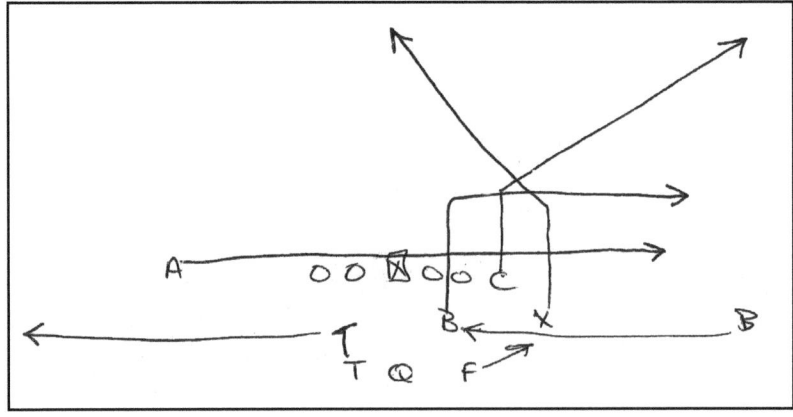

Diagram 7.37

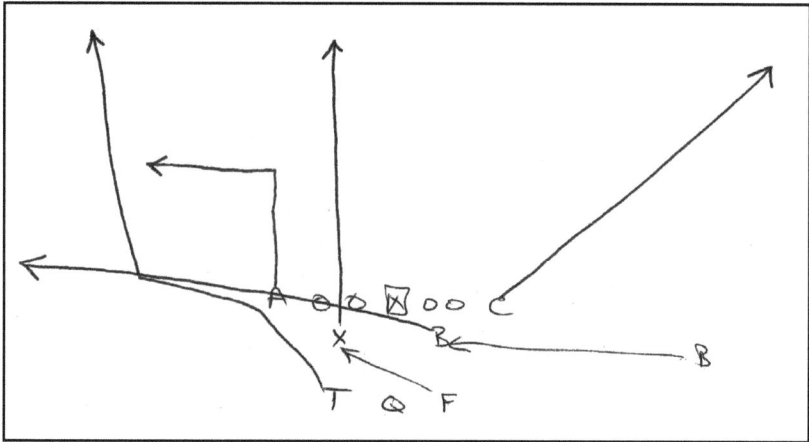

Diagram 7.38

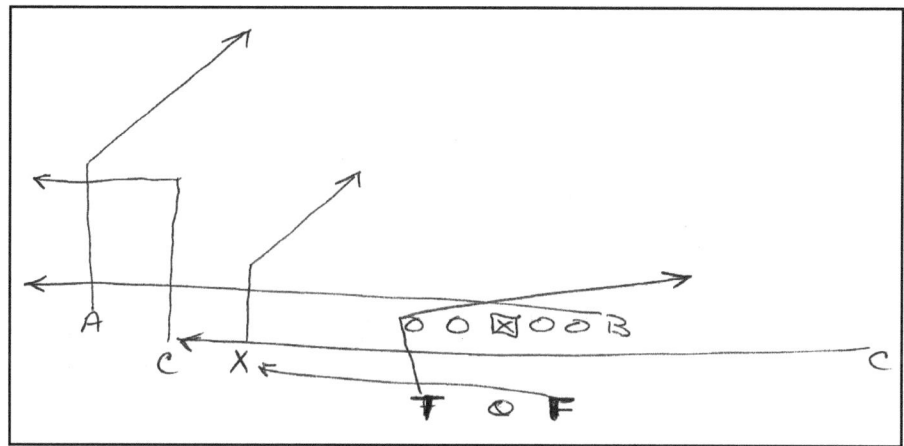

Diagram 7.39

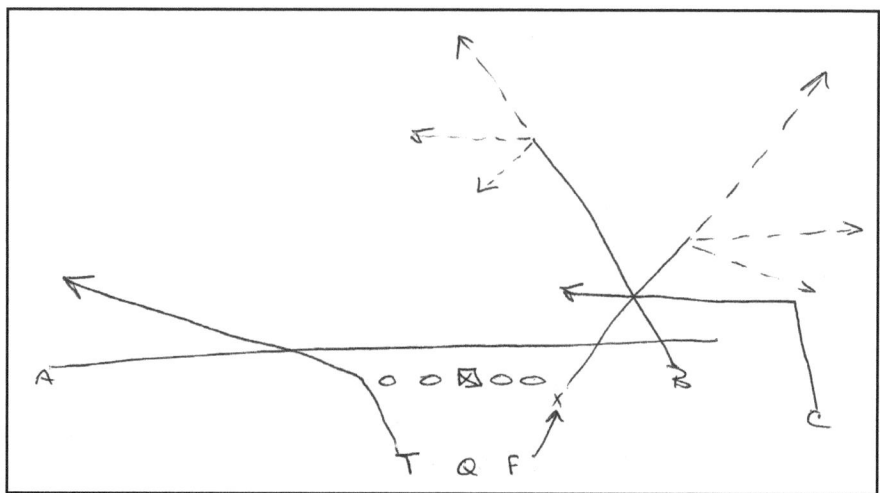

Diagram 7.40

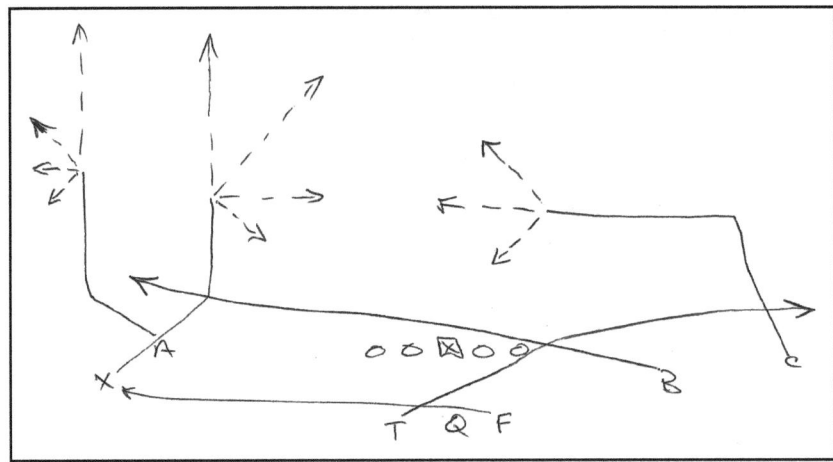

Diagram 7.41

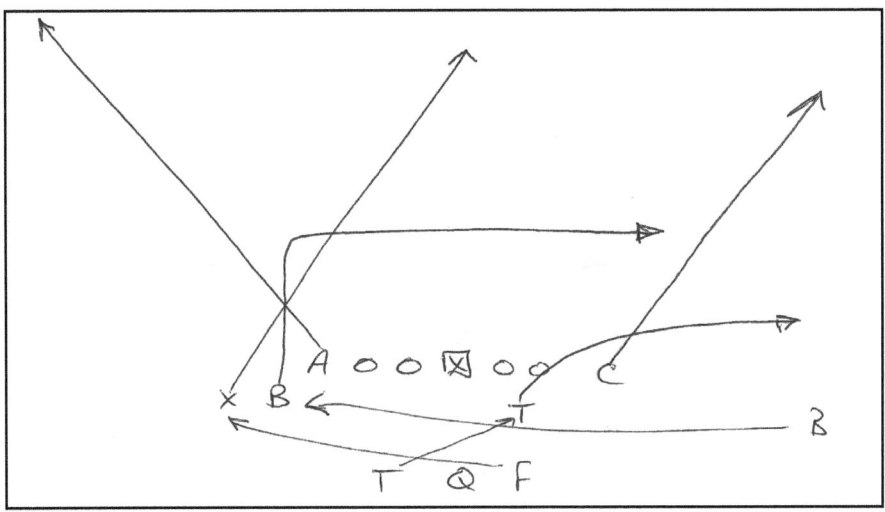

Diagram 7.42

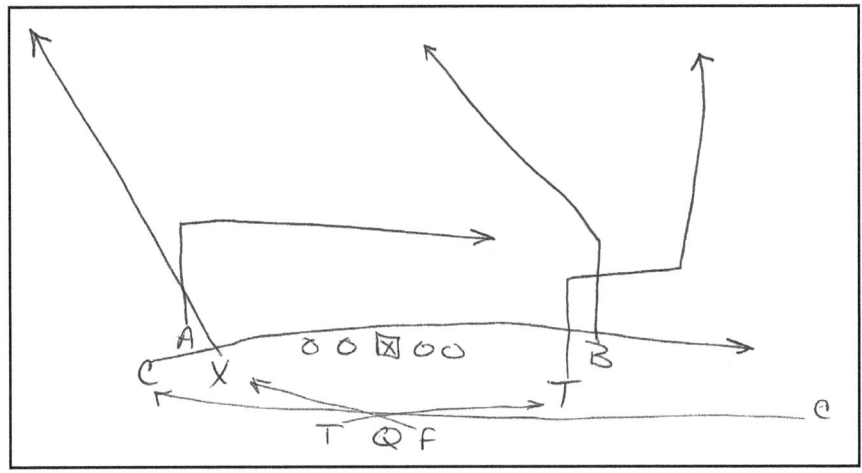

Diagram 7.43

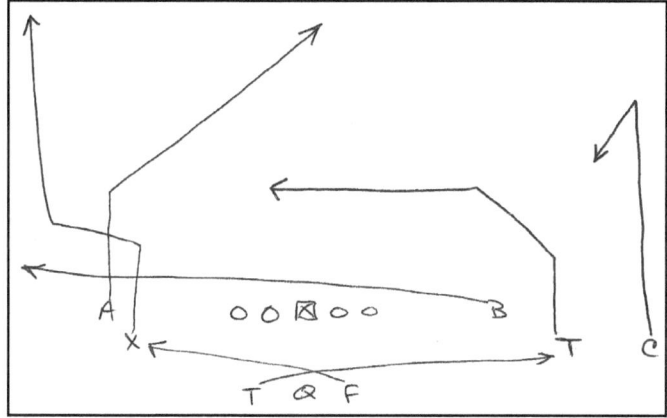

Diagram 7.44

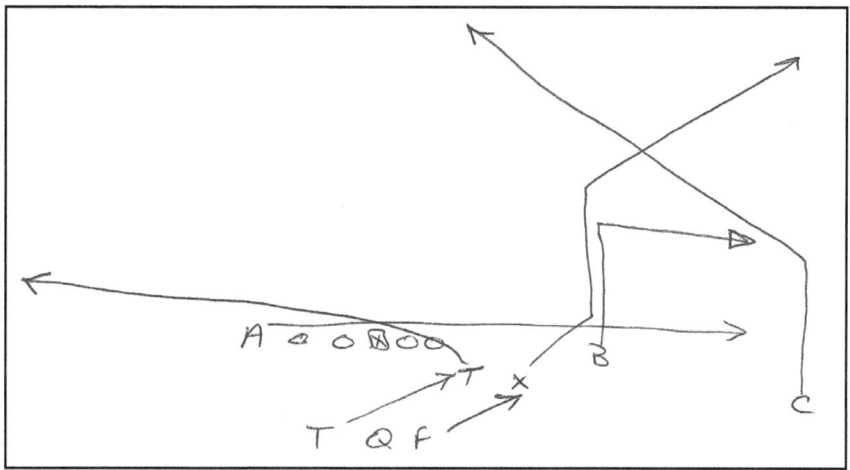

Diagram 7.45

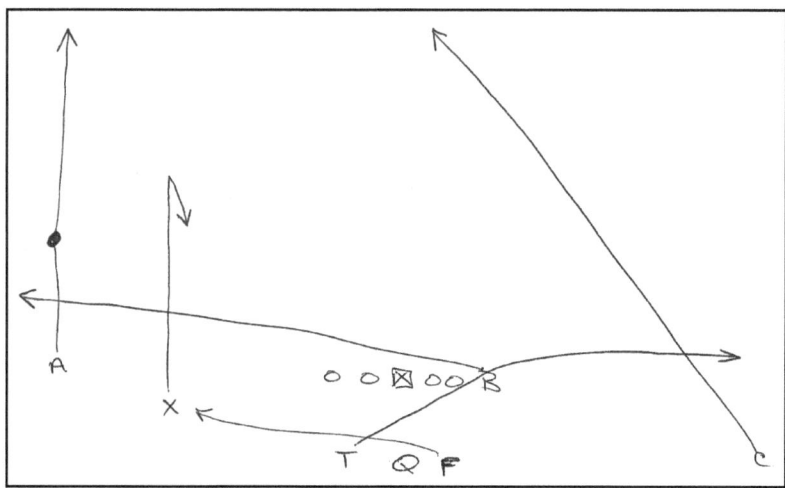

Diagram 7.46

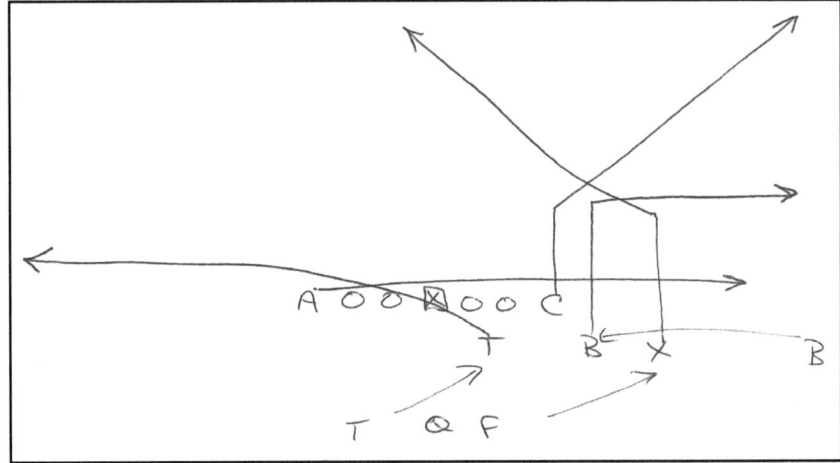

Diagram 7.47

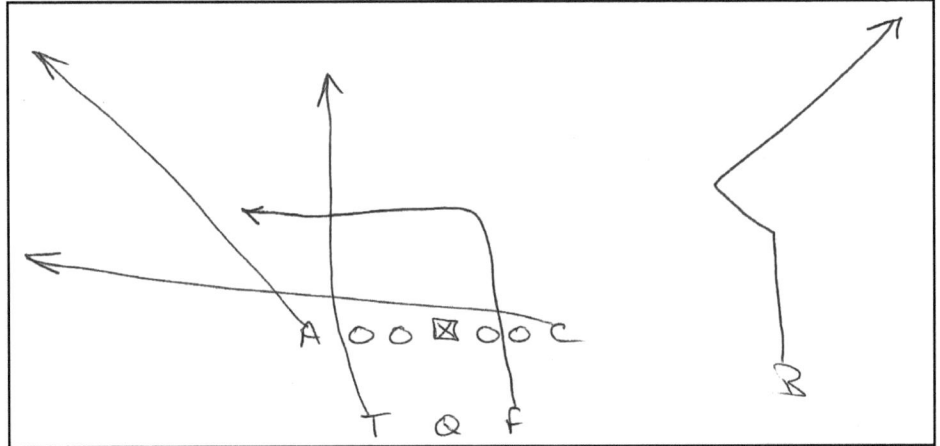

Diagram 7.48

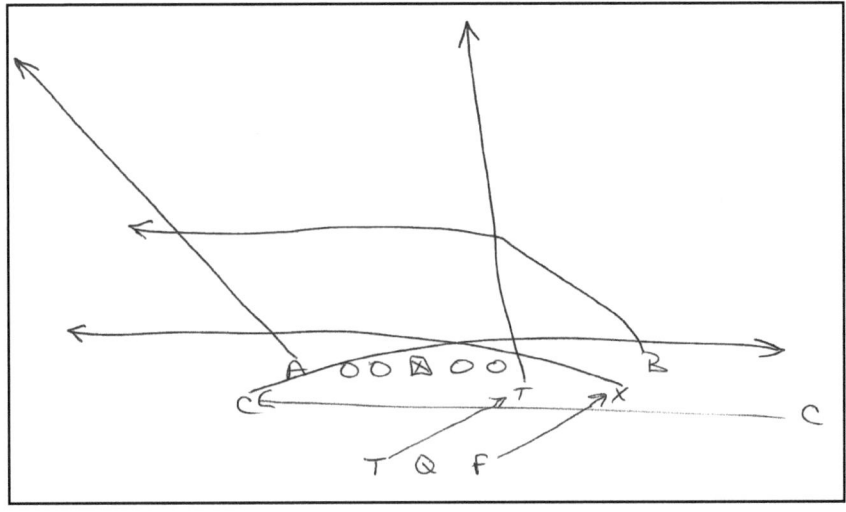

Diagram 7.49

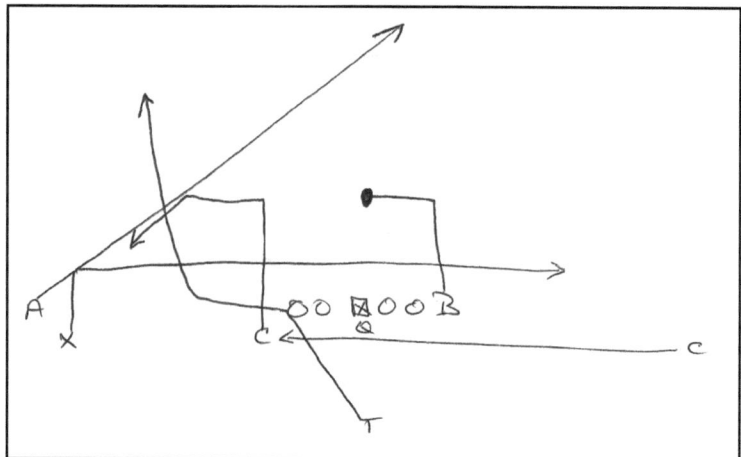

Diagram 7.50

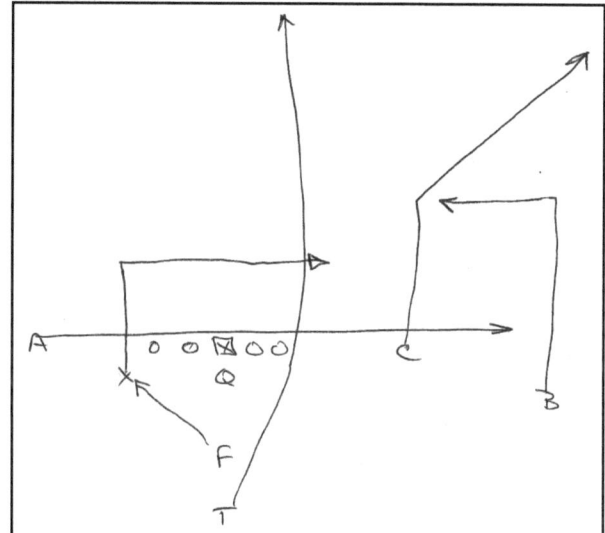

Diagram 7.51

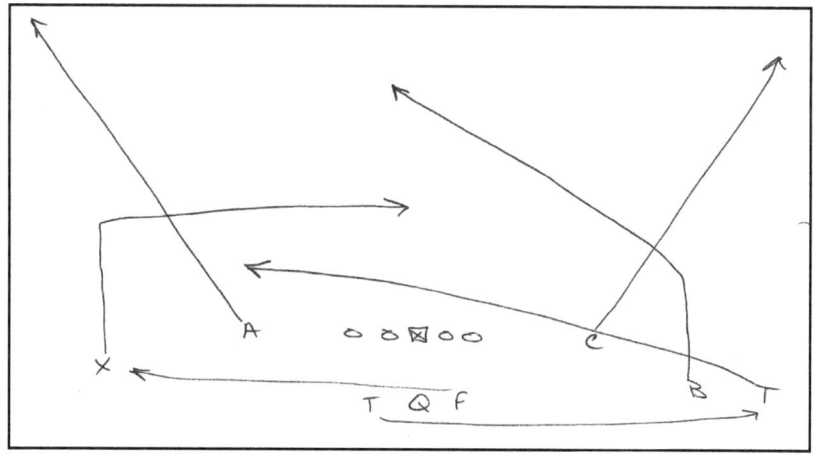

Diagram 7.52

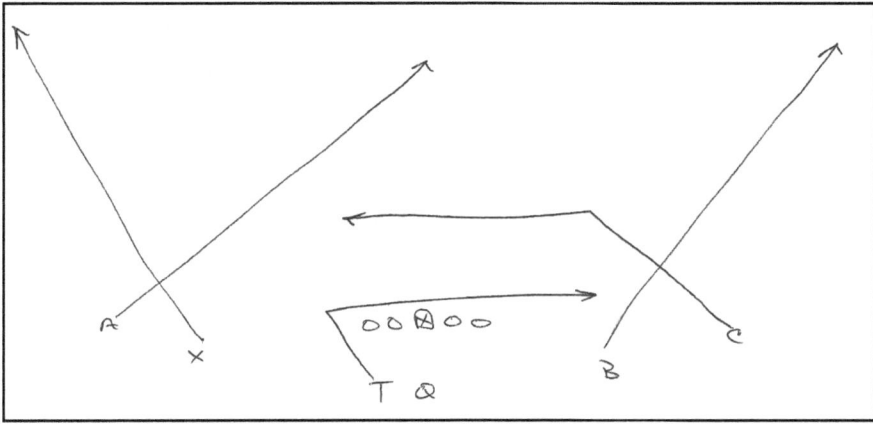

Diagram 7.53

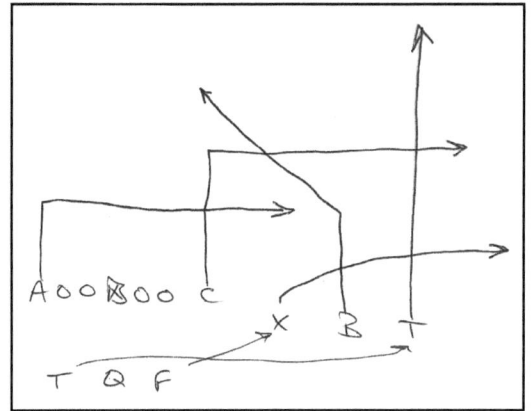

Diagram 7.54

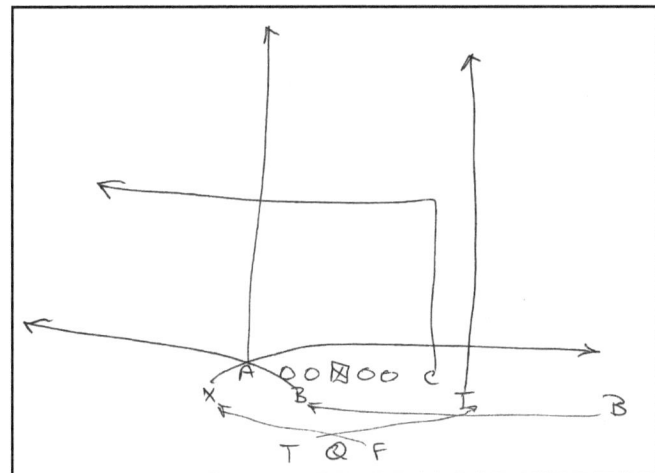

Diagram 7.55

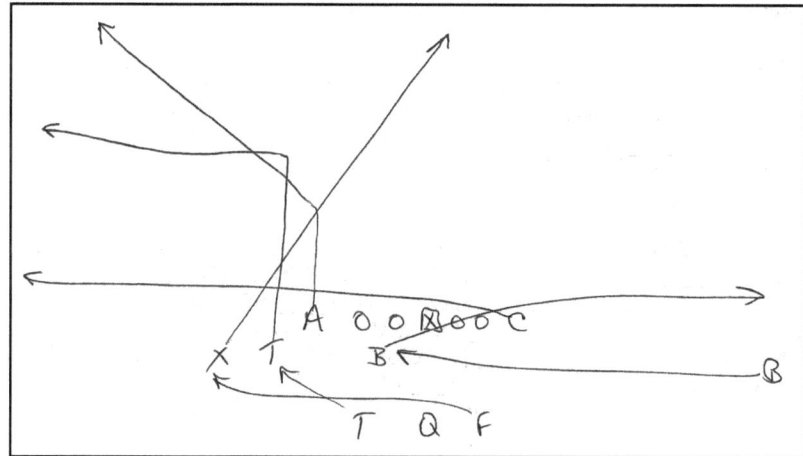

Diagram 7.56

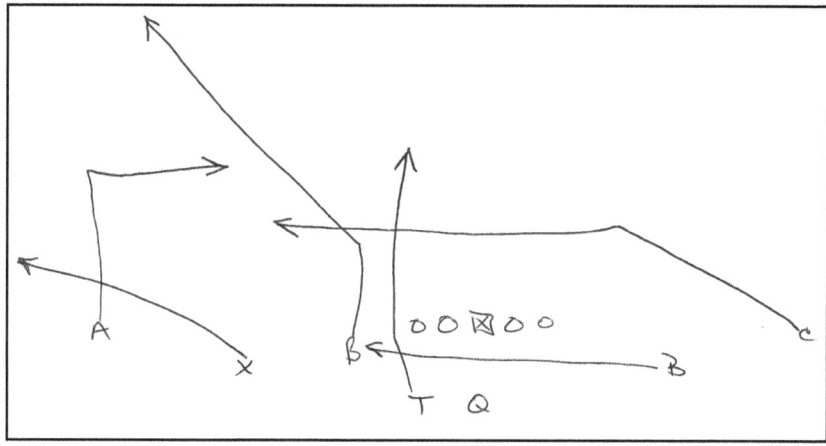

Diagram 7.57

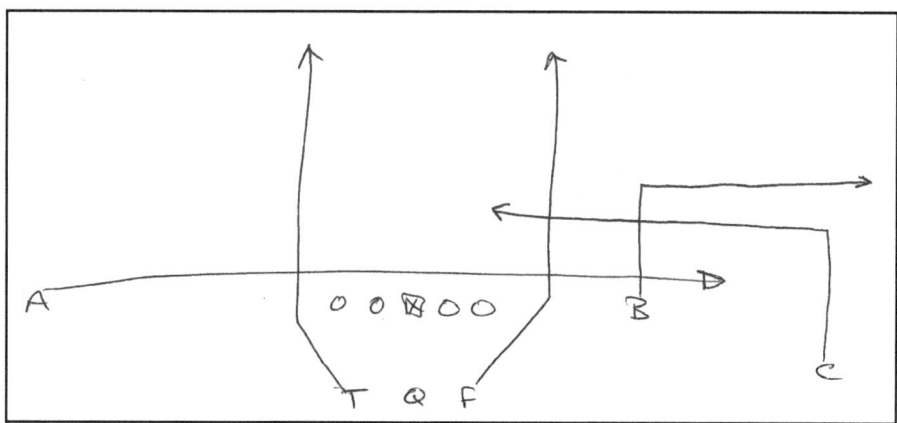

Diagram 7.58

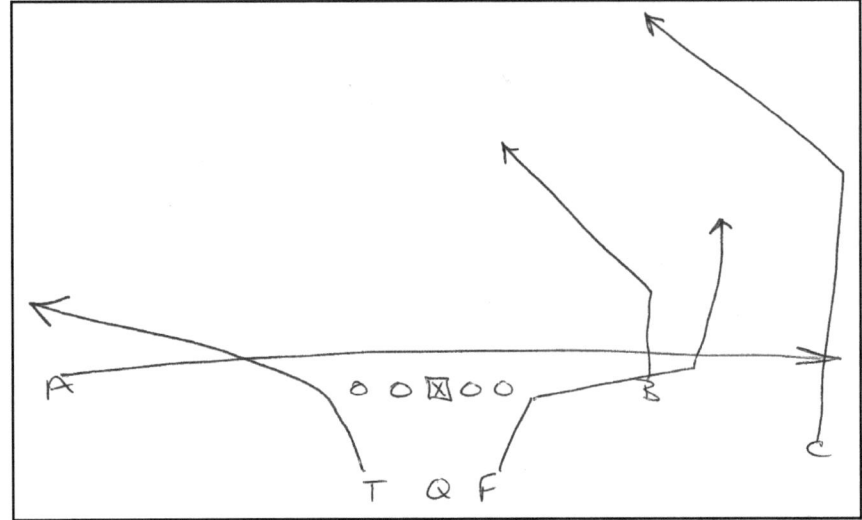

Diagram 7.59

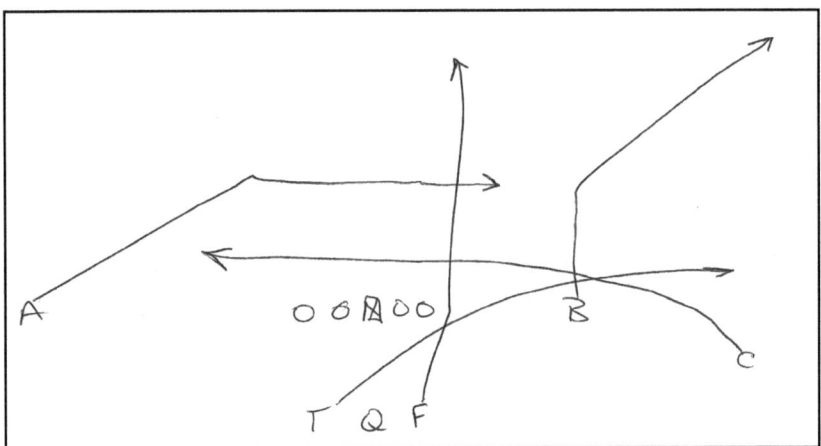

Diagram 7.60

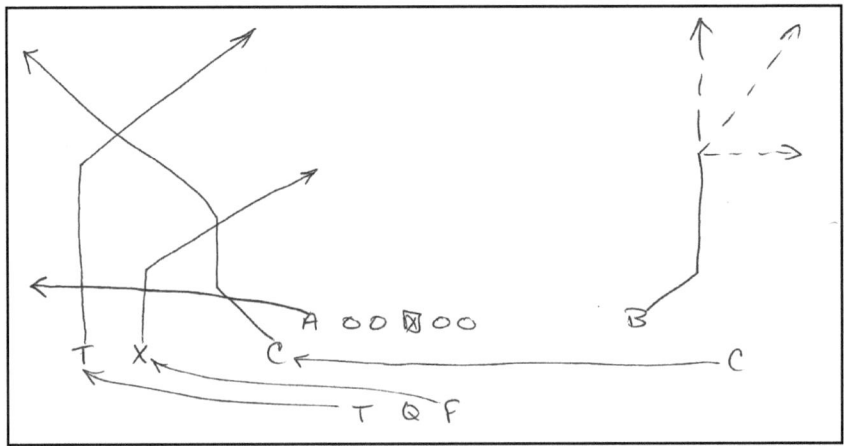

Diagram 7.61

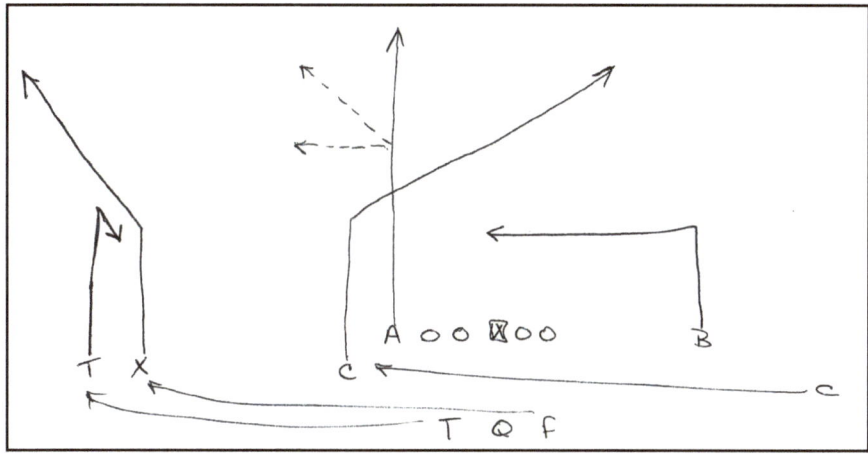

Diagram 7.62

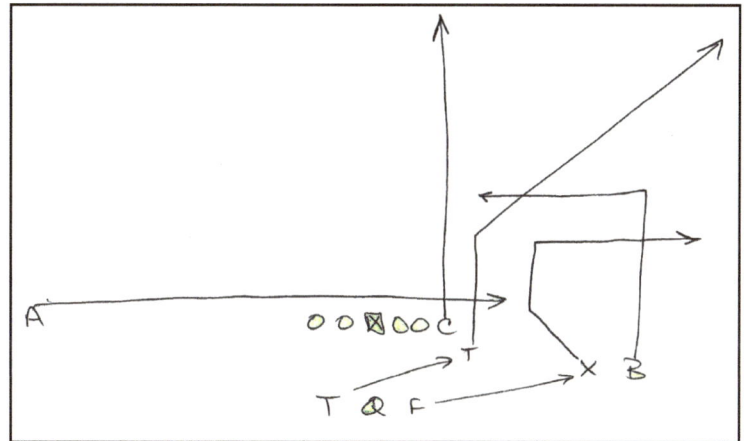

Diagram 7.63

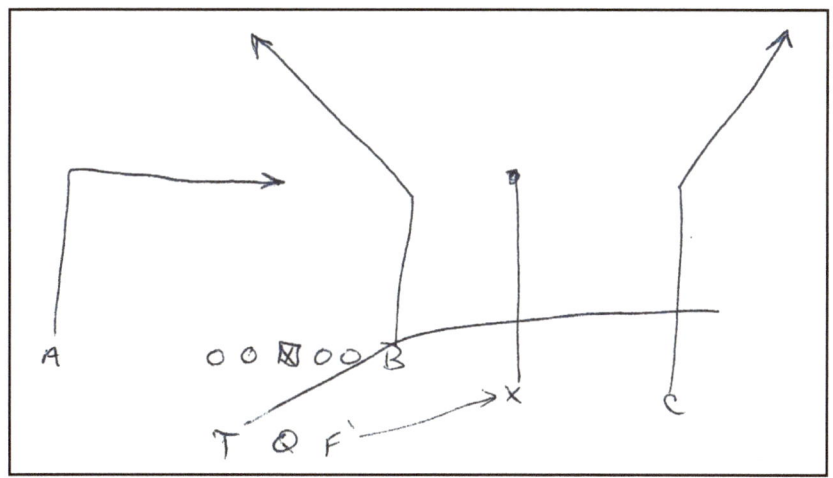

Diagram 7.64

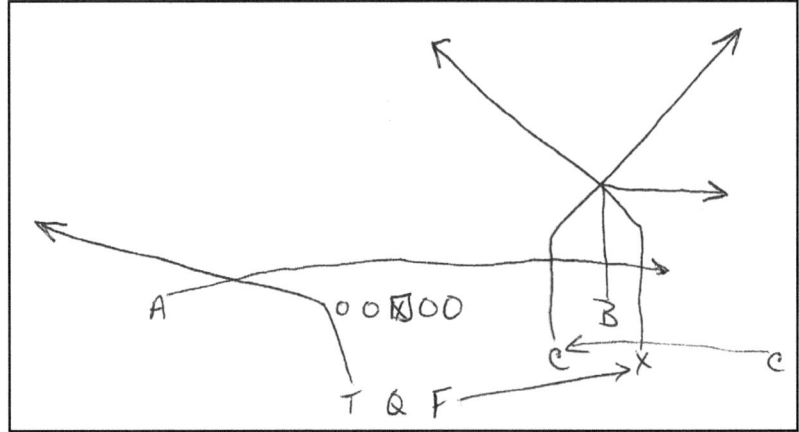

Diagram 7.65

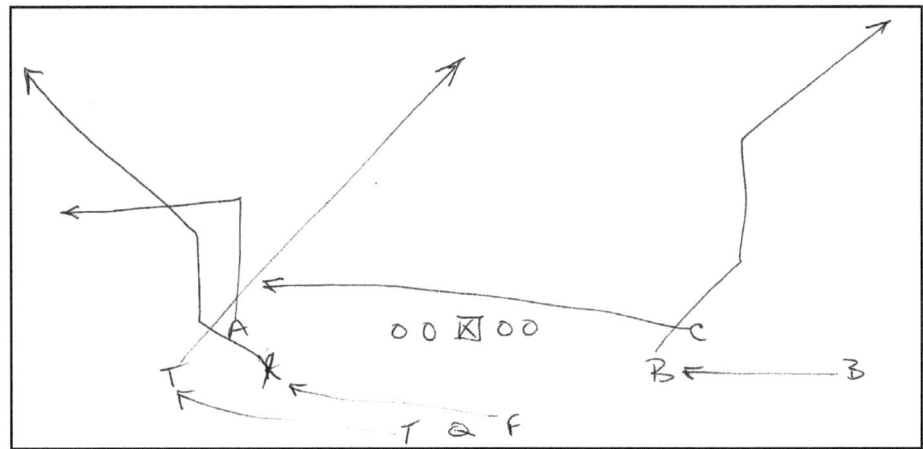

Diagram 7.66

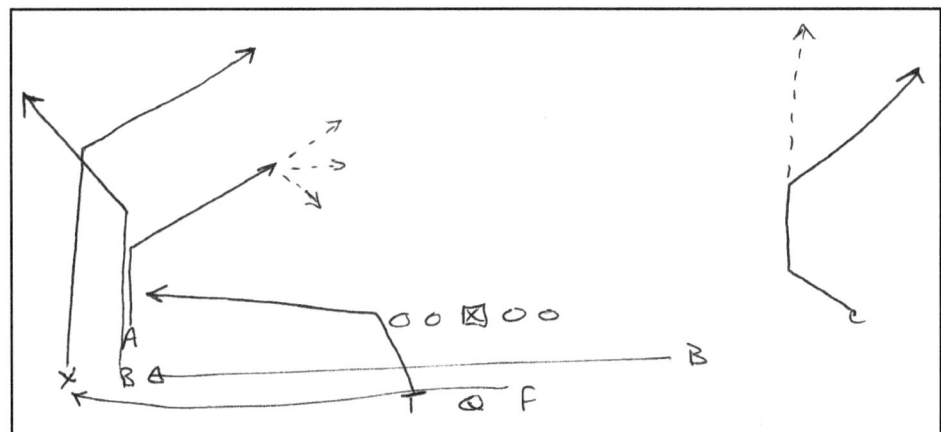

Diagram 7.67

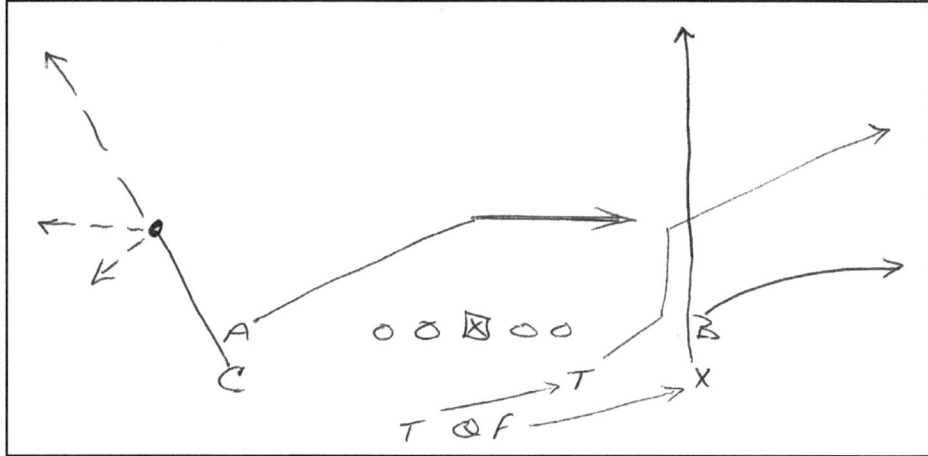

Diagram 7.68

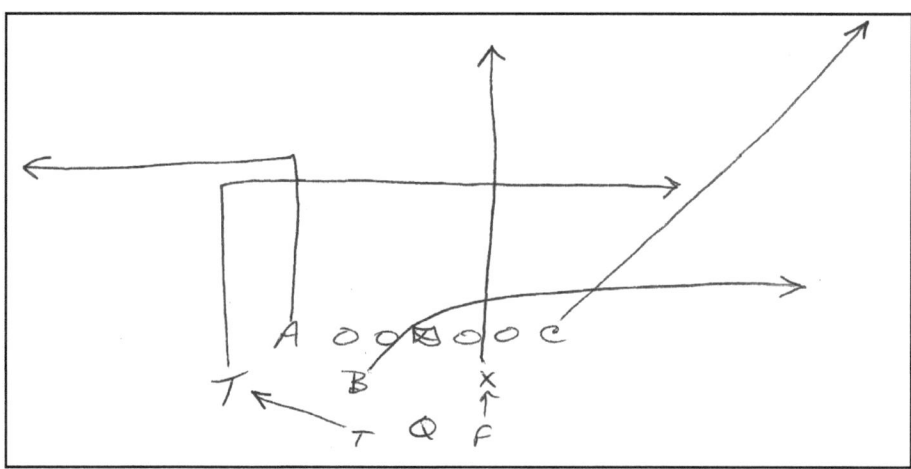

Diagram 7.69

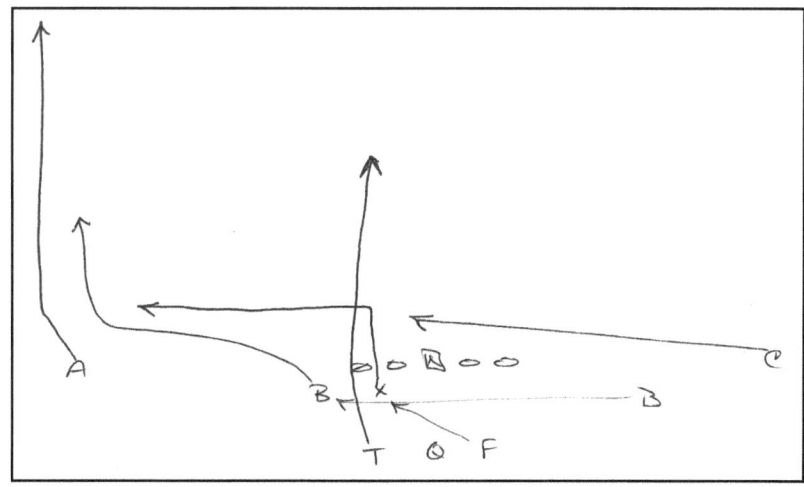

Diagram 7.70

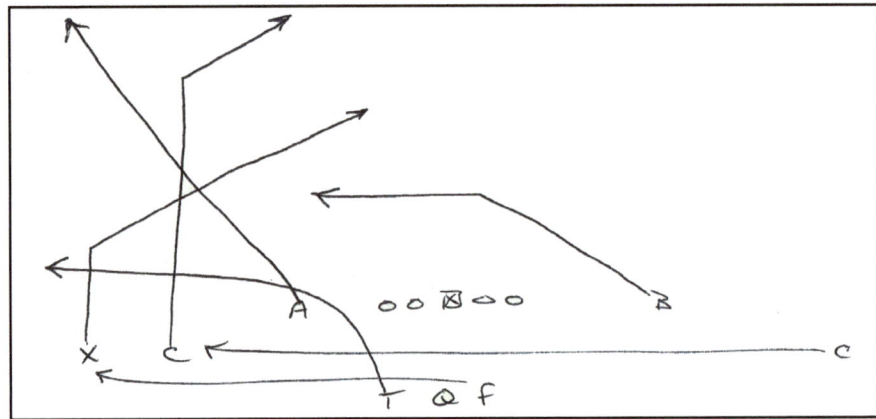

Diagram 7.71

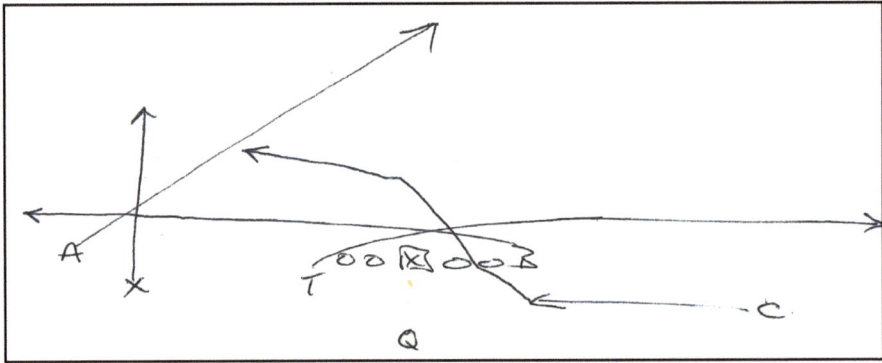

Diagram 7.72

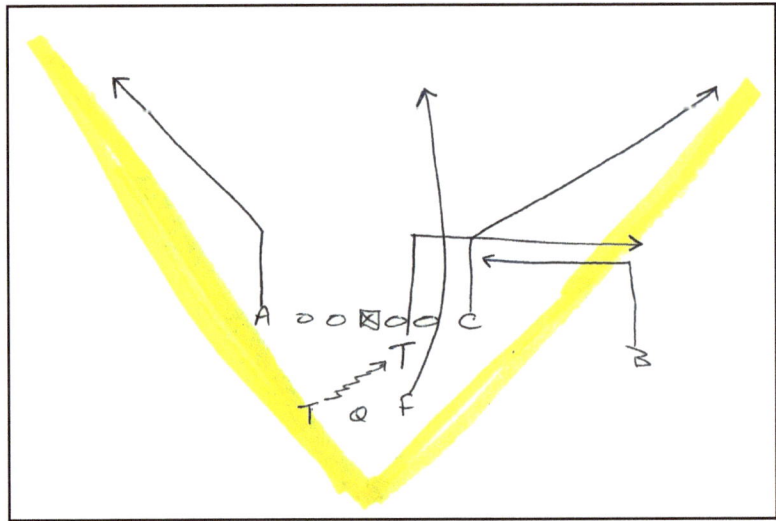

Diagram 7.73

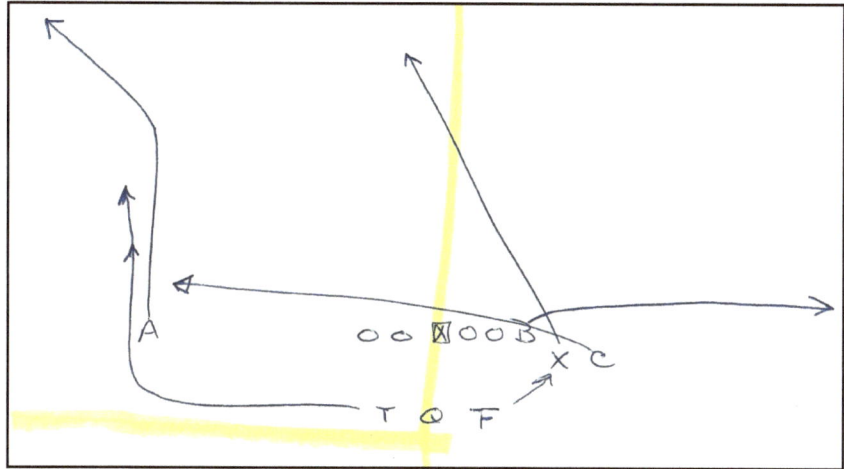

Diagram 7.74

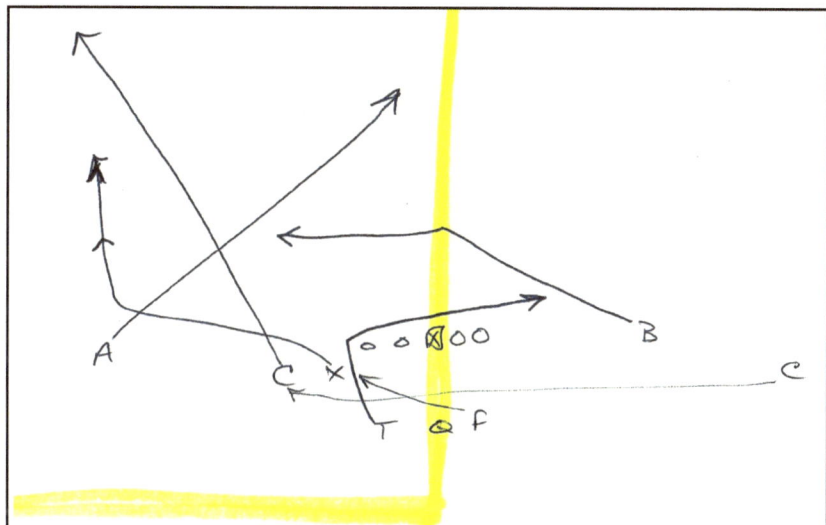

Diagram 7.75

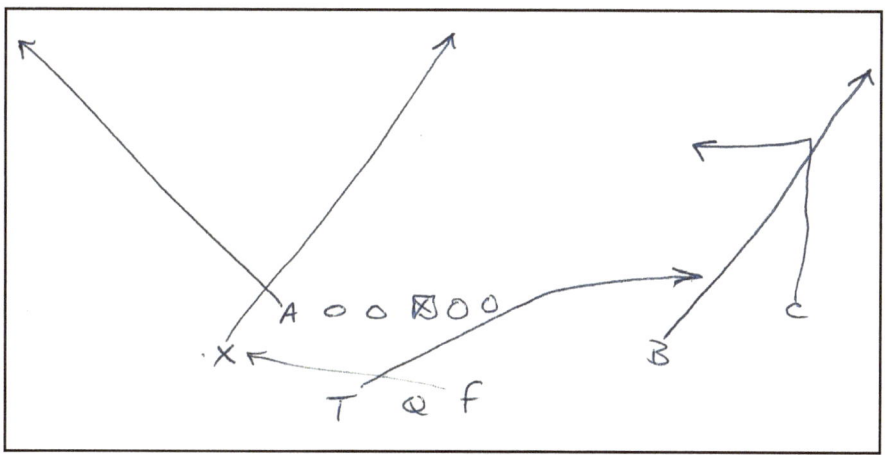

Diagram 7.76

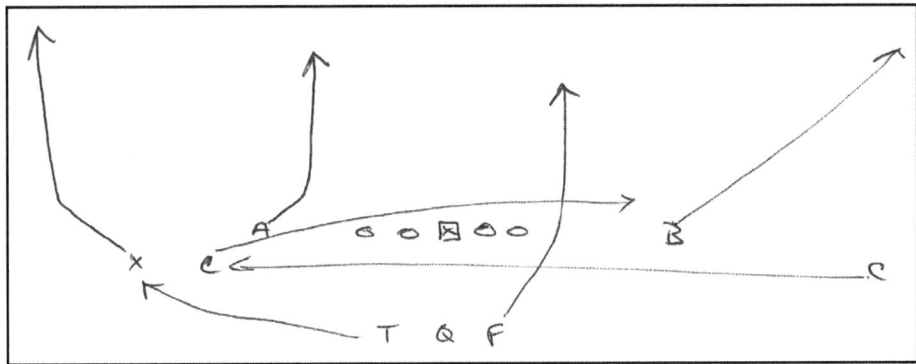

Diagram 7.77

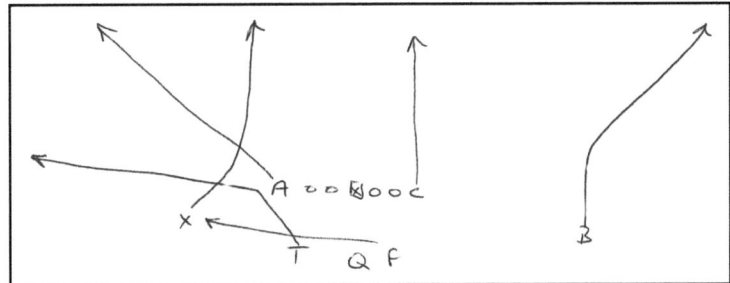

Diagram 7.78

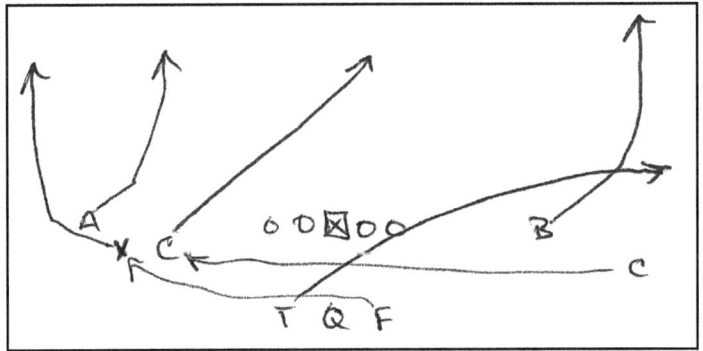

Diagram 7.79

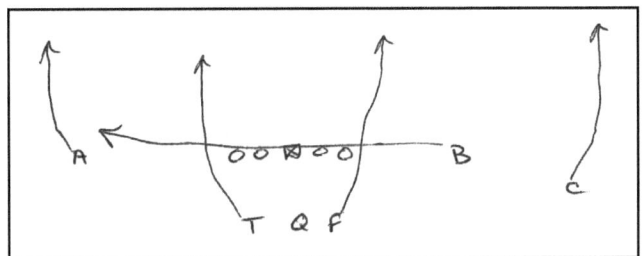

Diagram 7.80

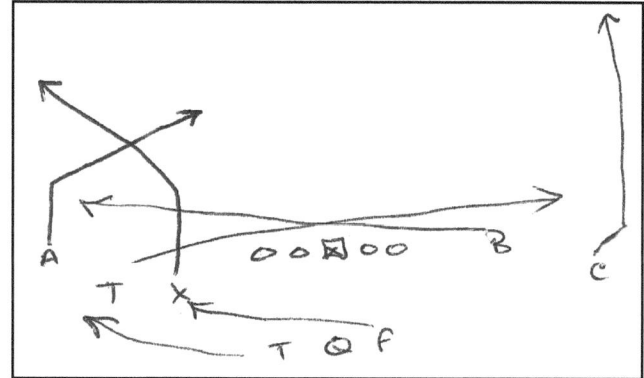

Diagram 7.81

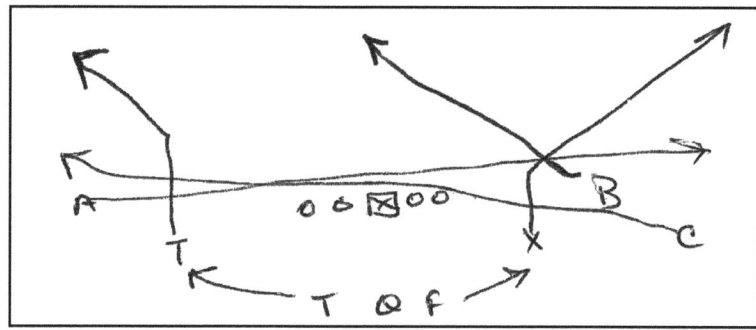

Diagram 7.82

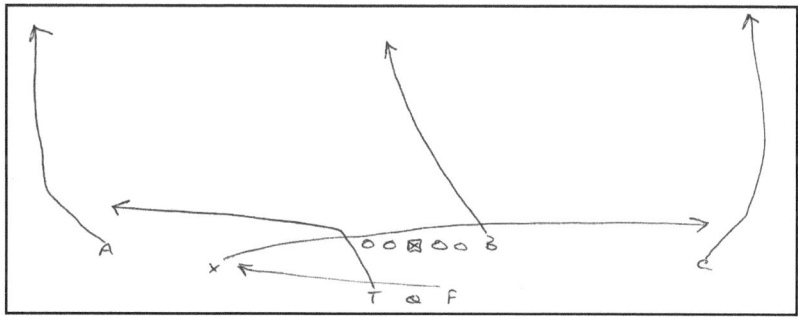

Diagram 7.83

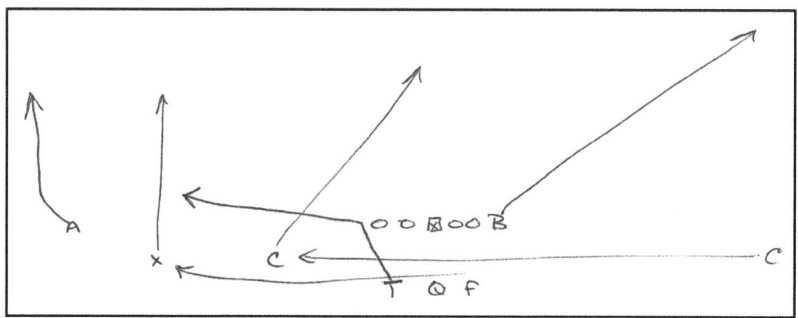

Diagram 7.84

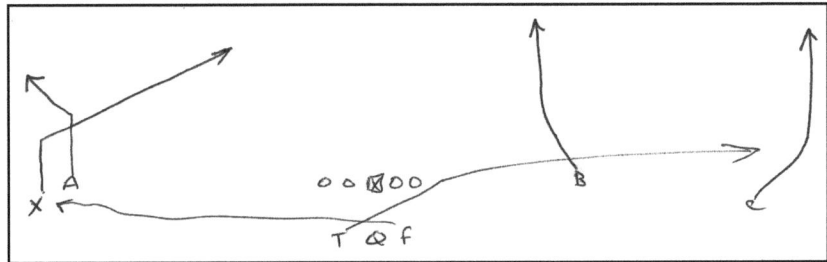

Diagram 7.85

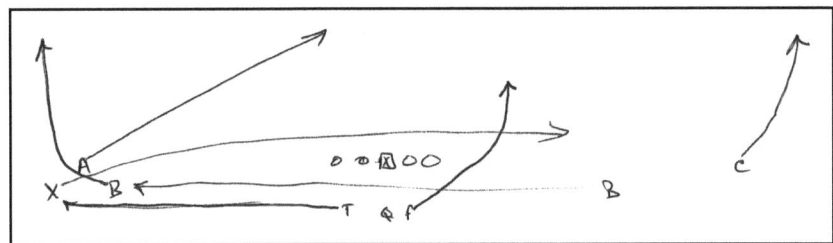

Volume 1 Conclusions

- Coverage skill is not the same at every level of football. I never use the NFL as yardsticks for my offensive ideology, strategically and pedagogically, for one simple reason – no relevance. There is no relevance between elite DBs and where I coach. That's not an insult or offense to our opponents. It's reality. I learned as a defensive coordinator that coverage is the most difficult skill to develop, even more difficult than quarterbacking. Two reasons why: uncertainty and unnatural. Running backward is unnatural. Not knowing the play is a great uncertainty. My defensive coordinator experience taught me that the road to elite coverage skills is long, slow, and painful. Without a strong pass rush in amateur football, coverage is no match for warp-speed no-huddle passing. None. Not even close. That's how difficult it is to master coverage skills. I never use what NFL DBs and LBs do in coverage as a measurement, guideline or influence about what I teach and why I teach it. NFL DBs and LBs are world-class elite athletes. There is no relevance between their skills and where I coach. If I made the mistake of thinking there was relevance, I would stick to a ground attack. Instead, I teach my QBs and receivers to never give the presumption of perfect or expert coverage. Again, no disrespect to opponents… just fact. My players' mindset is more important than opponents' sensitivity and hurt feelings. I teach evidence – video evidence that shows perfect, expert coverage is rare at our level. We don't expect it and we don't fear it.

- Pass rush skills are not the same at every level of football. Same as point #1. NFL pass rushers have no relevance to where I coach. The type of pressure we face is nowhere near the same that I see on TV. Similarly, we never give the presumption of perfect or expert pass rush. Again, no offense – just fact. I never have and never will cause our QBs to suffer excessive pass rush anxiety by giving our opponents excessive credit for pass rush speed and skills. Of course our opponents are good – but they're far from world-class elite athletes. Four rushers never have and never be will be enough to stop our passing. Neither have five.

Reason? Fatigue mismanagement. No pass rush has ever been able to stay at full strength against us when we successfully adhere to our 8-second clock.

- Overcome fear of passing. No passing system in the world will beat coaching fear of passing. If you fear the forward pass, you will show it. If your team senses you fear it, their fear will multiply. If you fear passing even minimally, no QB will fully trust the system, himself, or you. If you can't overcome the fear of passing, handoff. No offense, just handoff. A coach's fear of passing is the biggest obstacle, not the defense. Can you be 100% fearless of passing? Yes. Like anything else in life, unconditional faith doesn't just happen – it has to be practiced. More than words are needed. Passing tests your faith in your teaching skills, in your players' learning capacity… passing tests your trust in your training. So does going for it on every 4th down. So does going for two after every TD. I probably hold the world record for longest kickless streak. It was never a gimmick. It resulted in the most important lessons my players learned – never fear being different, never fear challenging conventional wisdom, never fear cutting your own path, and never misuse the work risk. Risk is reserved for life-and-death – survival. Not for a decision to punt or go for it. Not for a decision to kick a single point or go for two. I love football as much as anyone else but it's a game. And it's a stage – a platform to make an impact.

- Throwing mechanics is not quantum physics, not rocket science… it's **Pocket-Rocket Science©**. Throwing a football is a natural movement. I have never had a QB coach. I do it myself. I designed a 30-minute workout, a set of throwing and footwork drills that my QBs do every day during the season and as often as possible in the off-season. This 30-minute workout is applied during 90-120 minutes of intense practice where I use the concept of supersets and megasets that builds arm strength, accuracy, and focus away from the rush. It changes fear of the pass rush to the love of the pass rush. I call the 30-minute workout and the superset/megaset training Pocket-Rocket Science©. Launch rocket passes from a strict pocket but turn into a ball carrier as defense mechanism.

- Catching a football is a natural movement. I use 15-minute Target Practice, a set of receiving drills, followed by the same superset/megaset practice format.

- Pass blocking is made out of iron. Pass blocking is built in the gym. The *EXplode X Fitness Strength and Conditioning* system includes a sure-fire workout guaranteed to transform Point-Zero players into a hardcore protection agency.

- If a QB cannot handle pressure, nothing else matters. Not arm strength, not accuracy, not height, not 40-time, no throwing mechanics, not charm and charisma. Football, like real-life, will pressure you until it breaks you or makes you. If a QB cannot ignore pressure, the entire offense suffers. The team will be pounded and grounded and vice-versa.

- A high-IQ is needed to operate SWAT. Instinct Quotient… a special connection between QB and receivers. High IQ builds the beast, making a pass-oriented no-huddle into a high-tech air machine that can't be grounded. But high-IQ doesn't just happen. Nothing just happens. Our superset/megaset practice format has never failed to build a high-IQ.

To be continued…

Enjoy the book?
We would like to hear from you.

Post a review on Amazon, Goodreads or let us know directly at reviews@ginoarcaro.com.

Follow Gino & Jordan Publications Inc. on Social Media

- GinoArcaro *or* GinoArcarco.Author
- @Gino_Arcaro *or* @JordanPubInc.
- +GinoArcaro *or* +GinoArcaroBooks
- GinoArcaro
- Gino's Blog

More Books by Gino Arcaro

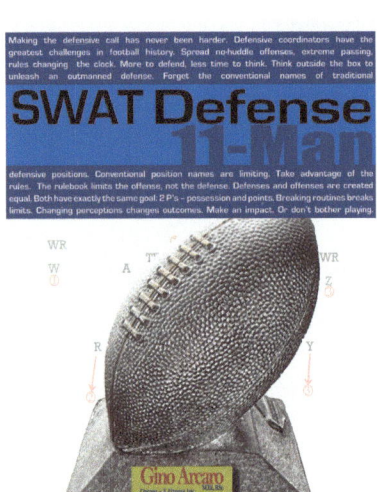

SWAT Defense
Making the defensive call has never been harder. Coordinators have the greatest challenges in football history. Spread no-huddle offenses, extreme passing, clock-changing rules. More to defend, less time to think. Arcaro's SWAT Defense shows how to beat the spread by forcing the offense to go deep and crack under pressure. "A stress-filled workplace for quarterbacks and receivers leads to an explosion." Central to Arcaro's system is his decision-making model that teaches defensive coordinators and players to make the right calls – those split-second decisions that have to be made about 60 times per game. Making the right call is not easy. Like any skill, defensive decision-makers need guidelines and experience to develop into full potential. A unique feature of the SWAT Defense is its ties to Arcaro's SWAT Offense.

4th & Hell Season 1
"We were David with a Canadian passport, failing miserably at winning just one football game against stars-and-stripes-draped Goliaths." It came down to fourth and hell – a face-to-face showdown. No disguises, no masks, no secret weapons. No one huddled on the sideline. No one huddled on the field. Both sides knew what to expect. No surprises, no guess-work, no mind games. Making the call was a formality. All that mattered was running the play to see what would pass. Someone would execute; someone would be executed.

eXplode: X Fitness Training System

Sought after his entire adult life to help others achieve their workout goals, Arcaro put his weight lifting theories and routines into this manual. His "Case Studies," true stories from his 40+ years of working out (completely natural) bring a sense of reality to the average gym-goer who just wants to get in shape, stay in shape, and most-importantly, not quit. No gimmicks, just discussion and formulas that can be tailored to any situation regardless of how long or how intensely one has been working out.

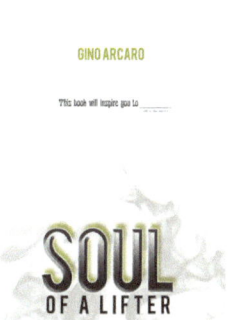

Soul of a Lifter

Gino Arcaro's journey from childhood obesity to natural health and strength was not made alone; he relied on the Soul of a Lifter. In telling this tale, Arcaro draws on life lessons learned from his careers as a football coach, police officer and college teacher to inspire and lead the reader in a soul-searching quest to reach his/her own potential. This is not your run-of-the-mill motivational book. Discover insights about what drives the soul… what happens when you listen and when you don't!

Selling H.E.L.L. in Hell
from the series Soul of an Entrepreneur

You may be starting out in business or just contemplating making the big decision. Gino Arcaro knows what you're thinking and wants to make sure you know what you're not thinking. His thought-bending tales, while entertaining and steeped in reality, will make the would-be business owner take a second and third look at the situation before jumping in. And, for those already "self-employed," Arcaro offers a unique slant on dealing with day-to-day customer and employee challenges.

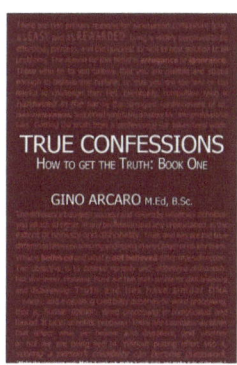

True Confessions

Gino Arcaro relates and upholds a simple fact: "Everyone has a conscience. No exceptions. If you're alive, you have a conscience. The myth of 'no conscience' actually means 'weak or dysfunctional' conscience." Therefore, a truth-seeker must appeal to the conscience, meaning, "make the conscience work out, make it work right, and make it do all the work." True Confessions is a manual for anyone whose job it is to get the truth. For example, Human Resources personnel during the job interview process or Law Enforcement interviewers who can use Arcaro's theories to open a window into the psyche of a suspect under interrogation.

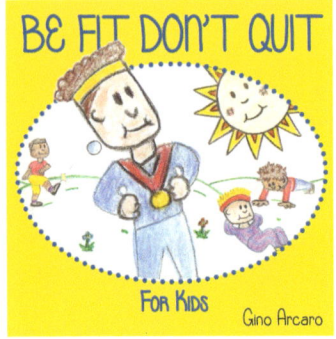

BE FIT DON'T QUIT
Full of exercise ideas young children can try on their own or with a parent, this book will rekindle in any adult a love for the simple act of playing. Gino Arcaro has spent his life working out and teaching young adults about the importance of "being fit." He wrote Be Fit Don't Quit to express a tried-and-true message: Exercising is natural and fun. Never quit!

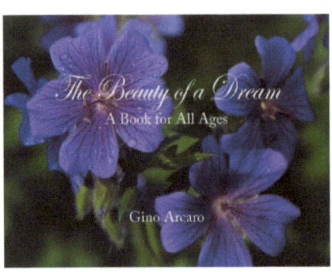

BEAUTY OF A DREAM
Inspired by the birth of his first grandchild, Arcaro wrote this colour picture-infused booklet to encourage the reader to dream, dream big and never stop dreaming. "No one can break into your dream and rob you of it, unless you let them." His message, in this book as in all his works, is a challenge for the reader to strive to reach his/her potential and make an impact in this world. A perfect gift for someone in your life who needs to be "lifted" or reminded that dreaming is important!

For more free book previews or to purchase Gino's books go to
WWW.GINOARCARO.COM

www.ingramcontent.com/pod-product-compliance
Lightning Source LLC
Chambersburg PA
CBHW040052160426
43192CB00002B/43